ALIGNMENT

ALIGNMENT

Overcoming internal sabotage
and digital product failure

JONATHON HENSLEY

with Dave Jarecki

Emerge Interactive, Inc.

www.emergeinteractive.com
www.productalignment.com

For special discounts for bulk orders, please contact the publisher.

Cover and book design: Lieve Maas at Bright Light Graphics
Internal illustrations: Damon Gaumont at Emerge Interactive
Photograph of Dave Jarecki: Rachel LeCrone, rachellecronephotography.com

Paperback ISBN: 978-1-7346604-0-1
Hardback ISBN: 978-1-7346604-2-5
Ebook ISBN: 978-1-7346604-1-8

Library of Congress Control Number: 2021905722

Printed in the United States

Published 2021, First Edition

PRAISE FOR *ALIGNMENT*

"Alignment is needed to create powerful product visions and fulfill these visions in nearly every organization. In *Alignment,* Jonathon Hensley helps show businesses how to effectively get aligned."

—Erik Qualman, author of *Socialnomics*

"*Alignment,* replete with logic and garnished with anecdotes, is a how-to for leaders everywhere. It helps drive home lessons around how alignment scales from the individual to the market levels. The book makes its case in the Malcolm Gladwell tradition, and shows that alignment is about creating concentric circles of growth. This material is something leaders everywhere can savor."

—Nishant Bhajaria, author, privacy and security leader, digital product architect at Uber

"*Alignment* is a must-read primer for anyone serious about scaling digital products successfully. Read this book and learn to connect all the right dots from one of the best."

—Gower Idrees, CEO, rarebrain

"Jonathon Hensley's book is long overdue. I wasn't aware of how many digital product transformations fail, let alone why. This book logically and effectively outlines the impact that alignment has on ensuring the success of any digital transformation initiative. The principles apply to any project or group seeking to innovate change in an organization. I recommend *Alignment* to anyone interested in improving outcomes, especially with development teams."

—Kent Lewis, CEO, Anvil Media

"In a world where customers are more complex than ever, Jonathan Hensley provides a new and invigorating way to pursue the desirous and audacious path of product development that actually leads to customer benefit. This pragmatic and digestible read will ensure you excel to world-class faster than your competitors."

—Hilary Corna, founder, Corna Partners

"Having helped develop two successful software products at SAS Institute, and a third product at Corios, when you are lucky enough to be 'in the flow' of bringing something successfully to market, seeing it thrive, and surpassing customers' expectations, it's a great feeling. But you are left wondering, what are the starting conditions you need, and the ongoing leadership priorities you exert, to repeat this experience? With Jonathon Hensley's new book, *Alignment*, we don't have to guess anymore."

—Robin Way, president and founder, Corios, author of *Skate Where the Puck's Headed: A Playbook for Scoring Big with Predictive Analytics*

"The perspective on the principal factor that determines the success of digital product transformations—human interaction—is simply refreshing. *Alignment* is not one of the many ephemeral, overstuffed pamphlets that get passed off as books these days. It's a practical, evergreen, and incredibly thoughtfully organized field guide to achieving repeatable success creating digital products."

—Mark O'Brien, CEO, Newfangled

"To create modern products, it takes a village of people with an array of skills. As a result, alignment is increasingly important in order for product teams to be successful. In *Alignment,* Jonathon Hensley provides a valuable guide on how to ensure your teams are aligned to increase your odds of achieving success."

—Dan Olsen, product management trainer, consultant, and author of *The Lean Product Playbook*

"Alignment truly only happens when everyone in an organization has a common understanding of the business value and differentiation for which the team is building towards. This common understanding only happens with time spent together and true empathy for the problem you are trying to solve. In *Alignment,* Johnathan Hensley lays out how to get your team from 'why me?' to 'why we?'"

—Randy Young, VP of product, Bugcrowd

"I find Jonathon Hensley's book, *Alignment*, to shine a light on the challenges that many companies face when they want to bring a valuable and sustainable product to market. From his experiences working with teams, he highlights key attributes throughout an organization that lead to a successful outcome. Spend a few hours with his narrative and I know you will see attributes of your organization that could use some attention."

—Mike Kruse, senior product manager and co-founder, ProductCamp Portland

DEDICATION

This book is dedicated to a few important people in my life.

To my sons - If the course of your lives leads you to becoming entrepreneurs and leaders, you'll have some of the insights and lessons learned in my life to help guide you.

To my wife - You have supported me in every aspect of my life, and without you by my side, our success in life would not be possible.

To my parents - I have learned so much from both of you, and those gifts have shaped my life. You've taught me to have a tireless work ethic, and to be committed to helping others, which inspired this book.

To my business partner - I am grateful for our friendship and the incredible business partnership we have built over all these years. Your unrelenting focus on growth, improving personally and professionally, and being a true global citizen are things I treasure. Without our work together and your support, this book would not have been possible.

To the remarkable people I work with - I have been blessed to work with an amazing and diverse group of passionate people. You inspire me. I learn from you every day, and am continuously humbled by your talents.

To the clients we serve - Where do I even begin? Thank you for inviting us to be a part of your incredible journey in the pursuit of creating amazing digital products and services, and providing value to the people that use them.

CONTENTS

INTRODUCTION TO ALIGNMENT

Digital product transformation changes the way business happens, and enhances an organization's ability to bring people, data, and processes together. When you transform a product, you improve lives, and revolutionize the way we interact with the world. Digital product transformation can disrupt entire industries, open new markets, spur growth, empower people, and create opportunities to engage, motivate, and inspire.

Through digital product transformation, companies and organizations can step back and revisit everything they do, from how they invest in internal systems, to the way they handle customer interactions. They can innovate incrementally, or take significant leaps forward. Digital product transformation can involve the next iteration of the iPhone, or the device that replaces the iPhone in the near future.

Of all the professional settings I've been in, nothing compares to being part of a passionate, high-performing, value-focused product team in the midst of a digital product transformation. When people possess a shared vision—and have the competency, leadership, and clarity they need to achieve it—the energy is infectious, and the results are usually spot on. The ability to create greater value, and make lasting impact, is evident.

How do product teams get there? How do they *stay* there? It's not magic, or luck, or chance. It's called alignment. When product teams achieve alignment, they discover and attain the clarity they need to create powerful product strategies, and fulfill the goals that matter to stakeholders, customers, and the organization.

This book is about helping teams and leaders recognize, achieve, and maintain the type of alignment that is essential to successfully deliver a great digital product transformation, and achieve continuous forward momentum.

>><<

Improving the customer experience, and enhancing operational agility, are table stakes in today's digital game. Having a commanding knowledge of strategy, experience design, and technology is a must. However, successful digital product transformation has little to do with the technology itself, and has everything to do with how people transform the way they understand and interact with technology.

Whether your business has been around for decades, or you're a digital native organization, the steps to delivering a successful digital product or service are the same. Yet, many organizations rush to change without undertaking the essential work that creates alignment in the first place. Without alignment:

- Your organization will struggle to effectively navigate digital product and transformation initiatives across the product development life cycle.

- You may not be able to create a great strategic foundation for your product that takes into account the sum of organizational voices and consumer needs.
- You may never be able to define an effective strategy that spurs buy-in, and informs critical decision making from a myriad of stakeholders, managers, designers and engineers.
- You may constantly struggle to level-up team performance to deliver continous, value-based results that move the organization forward.

Without alignment, your digital transformation is bound to fail. Still, only a handful of professionals are talking about its importance. Why aren't more leaders taking action to bring alignment to digital product and transformation initiatives?

To go deeper into the concept of alignment, and to bring this book into its own alignment, I spoke with more than 50 industry insiders, organizational leaders, product managers, designers, engineers, and team builders who are responsible for delivering internal and external products every day, and have been for decades. Collectively, this group has created value for hundreds of millions of users, and helped generate billions of dollars in market capitalization. Their thoughts and insights validate the following truths about alignment:

- It drives successful digital product transformation strategy, which is critical to identifying solutions and achieving continuous delivery.
- It informs every step in the process, and builds value.
- It creates measurable impacts and results.

For more than 20 years in tech, I have watched the business landscape change dramatically, worked with hundreds of companies, and supported digital initiatives around the globe. Through it all, I have seen too many good people and solid product transformation initiatives fail. Even today, I still see initiatives move forward without first achieving alignment, creating clarity, or building a strategic foundation. Organizational leaders are lured by the promise of innovation and technology, without understanding the fundamental requirements that guide initiatives to the finish line. Too many good ideas are left to die on the vines. People lose jobs, and businesses fold under the weight of unsuccessful digital product transformations.

A few things compelled me to write this book. More than anything, I felt it was time to share a critical understanding that too many organizational leaders are either unaware of or ignore—that true alignment requires clarity, focus, and a powerful strategic product foundation. When in place, these attributes drive higher levels of team competency.

Secondly, I have seen too many product teams grow frustrated in their attempts to engage in a digital product transformation. They're overwhelmed, and become bogged down as they juggle multiple priorities. To make matters worse, they often lack key information that everyone needs in order to collaborate effectively. They're in the dark when it comes to leading a successful digital product transformation that delivers a great customer experience, and fulfills operational needs. In many organizations, the processes that drive success either don't exist, are incomplete, or are terribly outdated. This book highlights what's missing, and what's required.

Lastly, as the volume of digital products and services around the world grows exponentially, leaders and teams must be ready to tackle an extremely complex ecosystem. This book will serve as an indispensable guide to help discover the way.

>><<

When people, systems, and business goals are aligned, product teams can focus on the right things, and take the steps that create strategic advantages. In so doing, they help organizations accomplish the following:

- Build a great strategic foundation for any new digital product or transformation initiative.
- Evaluate the strategic foundation, team structure, and outcomes of an existing product to support success.
- Generate clarity that's essential to strategy and team performance across every stage of the product development life cycle.
- Bring stakeholders, collaborators, and partners together.

While you can apply the various tools and insights shared in this book to any product or service initiative, we'll focus primarily on web, mobile, and Internet of Things (IoT) products and services. To help streamline the conversation, I have organized the book into five parts:

Part One focuses on what alignment is, and why it's so critical to the success of digital product and transformation initiatives. This section:

- Discusses what alignment means on the Individual, Team, Organizational, and Market levels.

- Illuminates how alignment surpasses psychology, and is related to our biological need to unlock natural creativity and problem-solving skills.
- Looks at ways that alignment helps product teams and organizations develop a distinctive strategic advantage.

Part Two provides a straightforward, honest look at why so many digital product and transformation initiatives fail or underperform. This section:

- Delves into failure and change, not just as concepts, but as realities that loom over almost everything we do in business today.
- Defines and discusses various paradigms that mislead digital product and transformation efforts, and the impacts they have on success.
- Wraps up with a look at learning from failure, and what is required to build competence.

Part Three explores what leadership in digital looks like today, and sheds light on the knowledge and skills that leaders need in order to navigate the digital product life cycle and transformation. This section:

- Focuses on critical ways of thinking when leading with alignment.
- Discusses challenges and common missteps that can impede performance and product success.
- Examines leadership's core responsibilities, and illustrates challenges that leaders must understand.

Part Four reveals the baseline from which every digital product initiative must start, and the elements and guiding forces that make up a strategic foundation. This section:

- Outlines the components that facilitate the creation of a strategic product foundation.
- Provides a framework you can follow to build your strategic foundation toward alignment.
- Discusses how to take action, solve the right problems, define success for stakeholders and customers, and measure your progress.

Part Five explores the connection between your digital product's strategic foundation, the core of your business strategy, and empowering team performance. This section:

- Sheds light on the critical roles that executives, product owners, and managers must play in order to build trust, and drive decision making.
- Reinforces the need to work toward solving the problem, not just falling in love with features and solutions, and what owning your product really means.
- Wraps up with team exercise starters, and helpful organizational models to support your digital leadership process and growth.

Throughout the book, you'll find anecdotes, stories, and insights from many industry leaders. In the **Acknowledgements** section, you'll find the names of people who dedicated time, energy, and enthusiasm to this project, often in the form of conversations and interviews.

>><<

Now is the moment for *Alignment*. Just think about the era in which we live. The internet enables, encourages, and demands that leaders say yes to digital product transformation. The landscape of the digital age is rapidly changing the way we manage customer relations, evolve brands, build value, market services, and ensure success. It doesn't matter if the rate of change you crave is incremental, focused on innovation, or geared toward disruption. Whether your business has been around for a century, or was born in this new era, the need for alignment is the same. To sit back and watch is akin to turning yourself into a dinosaur. However, to engage in a digital product transformation without knowing the right steps could bring about an even faster and more painful demise.

This book is for organizational leaders, product managers, and teams that are compelled to level-up, and revisit everything—from how internal systems function, to the importance of customer interactions, to the language that team members use when discussing a product. *Alignment* is for you if you:

- Understand that digital transformation is changing how business happens.
- Know that digital products and services are essential to your business transformation, but don't know how to get started.
- Have begun innovating the customer experience, and want support.
- Have an existing digital product or service, but you're stuck at an impasse, need direction, or are looking for actionable insights to move to the next level.

- Find it difficult to get teams and stakeholders on the same page.
- Are worried about falling behind, and struggle to finalize your product strategy.
- Have a digital product or service initiative that has failed, and want to figure out why.
- Want an honest, no BS look at what it takes to create a great product strategy.
- Want to set the foundation for your organization, teams, and for yourself, in order to create digital products and services that will make an impact, drive critical value metrics, and succeed.

To carry a digital transformation initiative forward, you must recognize and align disparate elements and groups. On one end of the spectrum, there's the alluring promise of technology. On the other, there's a very real equation that includes human capacity, available resources, time, opinions, experiences, cultural willingness, history, and a sea of unknowns. With alignment, you will drive clarity and focus through the entire process, creating a unified strategic foundation that establishes the prerequisites for success.

PART ONE
WHAT IS ALIGNMENT?

Four levels of alignment in product transformation
- Individual
- Team
- Organizational
- Market

A first-hand account of alignment

Alignment at the biological level

Alignment & building strategic advantage

PART ONE

What is Alignment?

"Great performance is about 1% vision and 99% alignment." [1]

– Jim Collins and Jerry I. Porras, authors of *Built to Last*

Alignment is the one thing you'll find at the heart of every successful relationship, team, and organization in the world. When developed and leveraged, alignment can create the foundation for unparalleled success, and unlock incredible advantages. Conversely, the absence of alignment can prevent the best ideas from being realized, erode the strongest teams, cripple the most effective leadership, and ruin even the most successful business. Yet, alignment is misunderstood, is often neglected, and tends to be underestimated in life, business, and especially in digital product transformation.

For some, the idea of alignment is that of a soft, steady voice in a world where people are encouraged to rush to action, and 'fail fast/fail often.' [2] For others, it's an elusive subject they only talk about in a quasi-mystical way, as if alignment happens because of happy accidents, stars aligning, or all the pieces magically falling into place.

In truth, achieving alignment is an extremely proactive endeavor that successful product teams and leaders focus on repeatedly. In part, it's the map you're following, filled with checkpoints that help you verify you're on the right track, or able to course-correct when necessary. When you unpack and distill the greater meaning of alignment—and how to achieve it—you begin to understand what it takes to successfully create digital solutions that empower employees, engage customers, optimize operations, and transform products or services.

Leaders in digital who understand alignment have a distinct advantage in leading their initiatives to success. They are more adaptable to navigating change, can more effectively address the needs of customers, and know how to increase engagement among their people. Contrary to what many people believe, alignment is not some soft, intangible, or elusive thing. It's extremely tangible, and one of the most important assets any business can have, especially when needing to move faster, and make better decisions.

Today's leaders know that their businesses need to be aligned at every level. Their vision needs to align with their strategy; their strategy must align with the organization's capabilities; capabilities must align with resources; and resources must align with management systems. Combined, this level of alignment is what drives performance. It also provides a path toward realizing any organization's larger vision with clarity and focus. What's more, it elevates team competencies across an organization's entire ecosystem.

FOUR LEVELS OF ALIGNMENT IN PRODUCT TRANSFORMATION

In the world of digital product transformation, alignment is the key to ensuring that an initiative reflects the company's broader vision. The most successful product teams work on four distinct levels of alignment:

1. Individual
2. Team
3. Organizational
4. Market

| LEVEL 1 | LEVEL 2 | LEVEL 3 | LEVEL 4 |
| Individual | Team | Organizational | Market |

These four levels provide an honest look at what it takes to succeed, from how to build teams, to knowing what will be required of organizations in the future. Such focus is common among impact-driven leaders and teams. Conversely, teams that are more production-minded—putting features and delivery ahead of creating value, for instance—will not succeed in the long term.

LEVEL ONE: INDIVIDUAL

Individual alignment means understanding how your work contribution matters, why you're doing it, and what the impact is. When someone is aligned with *why* their work matters, they are empowered to solve problems, develop clarity, focus their efforts, and make smart decisions. What's more, when individuals understand the larger context of how their contributions affect customers and user groups, and impact outcomes, their personal alignment extends into how they collaborate at all levels. This results in greater team competence, as groups can navigate the ever-changing digital product and transformation landscape together.

In too many environments, individuals expect leaders to provide them with this critical information. Otherwise, they will have to look elsewhere to get the context they need in order to do their best work. Without a greater context for why their work matters, people will fill in the gaps based on their own, often limited, experiences. When people make decisions according to their own biases, it can prevent team alignment from happening.

LEVEL TWO: TEAM

Team alignment is all about building alignment with others, so groups can move ahead together. It involves integrating unique disciplines, experiences, and perspectives to co-create, solve problems, identify new opportunities, respond to changes, and define a clear path forward.

As many organizational leaders know, lacking team alignment can be a significant challenge to overcome. Individually, people must fulfill roles and responsibilities, via specific capabilities, to produce outcomes. Whenever two or more people form a team, expectations may become incongruent. Here's a common scenario:

- Two people work together, but have different managers.
- Each manager has a different perspective, set of goals, and expectations for the digital product.
- Therefore, alignment must exist between the coworkers, and between their managers.

- To obtain alignment, the workers and managers must reconcile their expectations.
- When they do, they can align around a shared strategic foundation and understanding.
- However, if people put their stakes in the sand and refuse to budge, alignment will remain elusive.

The lack of team alignment becomes a shadow that lingers over every step that follows. It erodes contributions, hinders performance, creates silos, and delays decisions. However, when team alignment exists, outdated thinking evolves into a team-first strategy. Silos become thought-shares. Barriers disappear. Breakthroughs emerge. Once you unleash team alignment, you discover and reap the benefits of your collective potential.

LEVEL THREE: ORGANIZATIONAL

Organizational alignment deals with building alignment that reflects the organization's larger vision and strategic priorities. For a product initiative to be successful, it must mirror the organization's larger mission and vision, adhere to its values, and live up to accepted responsibilities. This level of alignment moves beyond unlocking the collective potential of a team, and unleashes the power of the entire organization across every function.

In *The Speed of Trust,* Stephen M.R. Covey talks about organizational alignment in the context of trust, its dramatic benefits, and the catastrophic costs of lacking trust.[3] Per Covey, organizations that are misaligned, or that operate without trust, run into a number of pitfalls, challenges, and even organizational poisons. To paraphrase a few of them from his book:

- People will manipulate or distort facts, withhold and hoard information, or work in a way that's intended to bring them credit, rather than work for the sake of customers, end-users, or the organization.
- People will spin the truth to their advantage, openly resist new ideas (unless they own them, of course), and cover up mistakes (rather than be accountable for their actions). Meanwhile, over-promising is the soup of the day, while under-delivering tends to be the taste in everyone's mouth.
- The blame game runs rampant. The watercooler becomes a fountain of hearsay and misinformation. People get sucked into sidebars and kvetch sessions. Splinter groups hold off-the-books meetings to complain about other meetings.

Have you experienced situations like these in your organization? Hopefully not. Instead, I hope your experiences resonate with the following list, which paraphrases Covey's take on high-trust organizations that operate with alignment:

- People openly share information, tolerate mistakes when they happen, and look for ways to turn situations into learning opportunities.
- The culture thrives on innovation, creativity, and collaboration. People are loyal to one another, and to big ideas. They talk straight, confront issues as a group, and readily share credit.
- Follow-up meetings become thought-shares and debriefs. Transparency is everywhere, as is accountability.

Throughout dozens of interviews for this book, everyone I spoke with pointed to just how vital alignment is in order to successfully deliver digital product transformation. It is also extremely difficult to come by. What I have found, and what others validate, is that establishing organizational alignment is the responsibility of every leader at all levels. That way, alignment among people, processes, systems, and policies can happen, resulting in high-performance organizations and cultures.

Covey cites organizational design expert Arthur W. Jones as having said that "(a)ll organizations are perfectly aligned to get the results they get." Covey himself states that "(a)ll organizations are perfectly aligned to get the level of trust they get. So if you don't have the level of trust and the high-trust dividends you want in your organization, it's time to look at the principle of alignment."

Finally, one of my favorite quotes on the topic of organizational alignment comes from John O. Whitney, professor at Columbia Business School, who says the following:

> "An enterprise that is at war with itself will not have the strength or focus to survive and thrive in today's competitive environment."[4]

To summarize, organizational alignment sets the foundation for the work to be done. It helps leaders, teams, and individuals focus on taking the right steps at the right time. It establishes a critical element of any decision framework, and empowers people across all levels. Finally, organizational alignment informs team success, helps everyone understand what it takes, and reinforces why their contributions matter.

You cannot take a holistic approach to digital product transformation without organizational alignment. It's paramount if you want to align systems, structures, processes, policies, frameworks, and people. Without it, you'll fall into isolating silos, and wind up fighting against existing barriers, while creating new ones.

LEVEL FOUR: MARKET

Market alignment deals with understanding customers/users, the problem you want to solve, its impact, the hurdles you'll face, and the recurring value that your solution will create. Whether your digital product is for external or internal audiences, market alignment is key. The stronger and more succinctly you align to the market, the greater your competitive advantage becomes. Moreover, you also set a new standard for the sustainability and relevance of your solution.

Of the four levels of alignment, market alignment tends to get the most attention. Countless resources attempt to unpack it, providing invaluable concepts, frameworks, and practices meant to help you define, validate, and strengthen market fit as you scale. However, rarely has market fit been associated with alignment at the Individual, Team, and Organizational levels. Understanding this context is essential.

To ensure that digital products and services are successful, and to maintain relevance over time, market alignment must be in lockstep with the other three levels. When you see and understand the connections, you are prepared to navigate market shifts, and pivot quickly when necessary. Your organization will be known for solving problems, and creating real value and impact—rather than being perceived as a brand that simply falls in love with feature sets, or chases fads. In this way, you will influence the entire competitive landscape, and inspire others to follow your lead.

Reaching market alignment requires organizational cross-checks, in order to ensure that the following occur:

• Organizational and team capabilities align with intended outcomes.
• Outcomes align with available resources.
• Resources align with the organization's digital maturity.

Whether dealing with a single team, or setting up cross-functional collaboration across an entire organization, alignment is key—from initial ideation, to validating market fit, all the way to scaling up. From there, alignment becomes even more powerful and essential. This is especially true when distributed teams are working on different critical flows related to your product or service, and the operationalization of each element.

If an organization's greatest asset is its people, then leaders need to do the hard work of articulating the critical context and information necessary to build alignment, starting with the people. Doing so brings clarity and focus to every initiative, empowers individuals and teams, unlocks their potential, and provides the foundation for success. In the book *How Google Works*, Eric Schmidt, Google's former CEO, and Jonathan Rosenberg, former head of product, talk about "Smart Creatives"—those who possess a triad of business, creative, and technical acumen.[5] In the view of the authors, one thing that's critical to their success, and the success of the business as a whole, is alignment. Their point is, whether you are a CEO, a product manager, or a member of the product team, the importance of alignment is the same. People need the right context and information to solve problems, or capitalize on new opportunities in the digital space. What matters for performance is how well these areas fit together—from the very foundations of strategy, all the way through execution.

Unfortunately, in most cases, people focus on only one or two areas of alignment. Doing so can be a cause or a result of the type of siloed thinking I mentioned above, and will come back to again. Compounding this is the fact that challenges magnify as organizations scale. The faster you want to grow and operate, the more important alignment becomes. With the unrelenting pressures of the market, coupled with constant change, you need to be an expert in navigating the unknown, and understanding the interdependencies involved in the outcomes you're working toward. If you undercut this understanding, the penalty is a high risk of failure.[6]

A FIRST-HAND ACCCOUNT OF ALIGNMENT

It's inspiring when alignment occurs at all four levels. Each person contributes with clarity and focus, while everyone collaborates to solve problems and unlock incredible opportunities. I have been fortunate to work with a number of aligned product and service teams. In one case, the client's goal was to develop an internal solution so teams that were spread across 160 countries, with members who spoke different languages, could collaborate and coordinate their activities.

At first glance, there were a number of challenges that could have easily led to failure. On the product team, close to a hundred people, distributed across multiple time zones, were going to be involved. Scope-wise, the initiative promised to be one of the most complex internal projects the organization had ever taken on. Despite these challenges, success was never in doubt, in large part because every stakeholder was committed to alignment. To begin, everyone agreed to the following rules of the game:

- Keep your ego in check.
- Bring your best every day.
- There are no bad questions.
- Great ideas can come from anywhere.

The organization had the skills and experience needed to complete the project—the rules above helped lock in everyone's focus. In addition, they understood the difference between leadership and management. Jared Spool, the founding principal at User Interface Engineering, has worked with hundreds of organizations for more than four decades. As he puts it, "Management is an appointed role. Essentially, the organization says, 'you are a manager,' and then they promote you. Leaders, on the other hand, are not appointed. They become leaders by inspiring others to follow them."

In business, some leaders *lead* people, while others *manage* things. True leaders must encourage people to buy into a big idea, and carry it through to the end. In the scenario above, our client created a clear, strategic foundation, and built alignment that started on the individual level. People and teams were engaged and excited about taking on challenges, and moving past stumbling blocks they encountered along the way. The environment became highly collaborative, and the entire process became a co-creative experience.

You could see enthusiasm manifest in meetings and work sessions. Teams solved critical problems, explored possibilities, and tested assumptions before committing to a direction.

They also kept in mind the many intricacies involved in supporting users, managers, and leadership. As people continued to work from alignment, they built authentic and meaningful relationships, and left nothing to chance. The pace of their work accelerated, and quality increased at each step.

In the end, we were able to manage and meet stakeholders' expectations on time and on budget. We were also able to transfer the institutional knowledge developed through the process to their internal teams, so they could execute and roll out the product across the organization. Of critical importance, we defined a clear, strategic foundation and roadmap, not just a list of features. The roadmap included opportunities the client could unlock incrementally to support their broader focus, while staying flexible in the face of evolving business demands. This would not have been possible without alignment at each of the four levels (Individual, Team, Organizational, and Market), and the shared commitment to staying focused on solving key challenges, without falling in love with any single solution too soon.

The project stayed true to the value and impact that the client needed. The result was a solution they could improve upon over time thanks to continuous discovery and product iteration.

ALIGNMENT AT THE BIOLOGICAL LEVEL

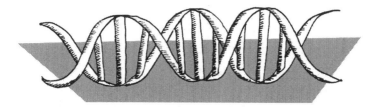

Has organizational alignment always been so important? No. During the Industrial Revolution, for instance, workers didn't need to possess a deeper understanding of what they were doing. They broke their days down into small, repeatable tasks. In factories, shop floors, mines, and assembly lines, siloing knowledge and information was the norm. Workers at various stations put the screws where they needed to go, and didn't worry about the rest of whatever was being built.

Things do not work this way in a digital era. In fact, at a time when digital technology is ubiquitous and essential to nearly every business, old approaches, methodologies, and frameworks are outdated and obsolete. However, while change sometimes happens rapidly, changing minds, attitudes, and the way people work can be slow.

An interesting aspect about alignment is that it's an innate psychological and physiological desire. We all seek alignment. As professionals, we want to know how our work matters. We care about the purpose behind what we do, and find the relationship between cause and effect important. However, this desire can become muted when we're stuck in traditional structures that enforce outdated ways of thinking and working.

Dan Cable, a leading neuroscientist, and professor of organizational behavior at London Business School, talks about this biological thirst for alignment in his book, *Alive at Work.* When we spoke, he shared a number of remarkable insights that approach alignment from a deeper, biological level, beginning with the idea of self-verification. According to Cable, this is another way of saying that the people around here know and care about who I really am.

"It's a very personal and psychological type of understanding that relates to how people see themselves, and how they believe others see them," he says. From this perspective, a person who feels they are in a place where others see their true self might feel compelled to bring this true self to work every day—rather than pretend in order to get along. "For them, work is a place where they feel accepted," he says. "They belong because of who they are."

There's a lot of literature that suggests how this mindset can open people up to offer a unique perspective only they can share. They feel confident to try things in different ways. Even though others around them might be focused on X, they know there's room to try Y. In any organization, this level of freedom can lead to more creativity, innovation, and experimentation. It can also strengthen workgroups where people don't feel stymied, or won't get defensive about their decisions.

"They're not always trying to one-up each other in team meetings," Cable says. "Instead, they're trying to share information to solve a common problem, which becomes a thing that's *out there*, not *in here among us.*"

Moving beyond self-verification, the other biological aspect of alignment is more organizational, or team-based. It speaks to the idea of possessing a shared understanding of *why we're all here*, which boils down to the notion of working together to solve problems. As Cable says, "We understand and agree that there is a problem we're all trying to fix, and that's why we're here. Sometimes, that means we're going to try a problem-solving approach no one has tried before. Whether it works or not, we're in it together."

This team-based notion points back to the idea of experimentation—when a group of people understand the challenge, and are aligned in an effort to solve it, they can experiment and explore possibilities together. In the digital space, when certain solutions might not last more than a year, it's vital to build and maintain an environment where groups can work synergistically, understanding as a unit what's at stake, and how each step feeds the next. This is in sharp contrast to an outdated model where individuals do not know, understand, or even care about the bigger purpose of their work. In an aligned environment, leaders give people the tools they need to understand what they're building, and empower them to adapt when called upon to do so.

When self-verification, and a collective understanding coalesce in the digital space, it drives a sense of purpose that impacts the four levels we've been focusing on (Individual, Team, Organizational, and Market). "In many cases," Cable says, "people frame this understanding around agreeing on why they're here. I think the part that offers the most unique perspective relates to personalizing *why me*, while still agreeing with *why we*."

For leaders, being able to drive alignment involves bridging the 'why me/why we' gap, and rallying people around purpose. Doing so takes much more than simply regurgitating a well-crafted mission statement. "Instead of actually driving agreement and alignment," Cable says, "too many leaders often sound like this: 'You all heard my talk where I discussed our purpose. Now go make it happen.' They think that if they craft and distribute the right combination of words, everyone will suddenly tune in and get excited. That's not the way."

Cable cites the work of Jaak Panksepp. An Estonian neuroscientist, Panksepp coined the phrase 'affective neuroscience,' which became the name for the field that studies the neural mechanisms of emotion.[7] Panksepp's work goes into great detail about the biology associated with certain emotions, including what the brain is looking for in different types of engagements and scenarios.

"Recognizing cause and effect isn't unique to humans," Cable says. "It occurs in all mammals. There's an urge to discover what happens when we act a certain way. 'How will the environment respond if I press this button? Will I get rewarded? Let's see.'"

Our bodies are built to try new things, explore, and discover how our actions affect and impact the world around us. For instance, pressing the button might release a shot of dopamine, which gives us an energizing jolt as part of the body's built-in reward system. "Cause and effect bring about purpose," Cable says. "Now, when you point this back to an organization, who gets rewarded? What does it look like when we do a really good job?"

When leaders try to arrive at these answers through words, but not actions, people don't experience them at a personal level. They're not discovering what happens when they press this or that button. They're missing out on the critical transfer of cause-and-effect data, and have no way of seeing themselves or their work within the larger narrative of 'why me/why we.' However, when leaders align the group's purpose with individual efforts, people experience the results of their actions. The larger 'we' purpose goes from being something written or said, to an experience that people feel on a personal level. They readily envision their part in the process, and understand the role they play in the organization's success.

"Purpose must be something that people feel through experience," Cable adds. "It's not just logical, but also emotional." This can be a stumbling block for many leaders, especially if they're only focused on communicating the message, but don't empower people to take action, and thereby live the experience.

ALIGNMENT & BUILDING STRATEGIC ADVANTAGE

To realize alignment, and the strategic advantage that comes with it, leaders must rethink how they approach strategy. Doing so prepares them for challenges, and sets the stage to deliver results that encourage innovation, engage new generations of problem solvers, and increase the quality, efficiency and effectiveness of the work that happens organizationally.

For many leaders, it's counterintuitive to think of themselves as being *less* important than their workers are, or accept that their job is to serve their employees. However, when you truly explore what goes on inside an organization, it becomes clear that the people who produce work—strategists, researchers, designers, programmers, customer representatives, and marketers—add the greatest value to every endeavor. In Dan Cable's view, leaders can only add value if they're helping their people do the same.

"Your job is to serve them as they add value," he says. "Some leaders can't even consider this thought. It's an insult to them. They feel threatened." However, when leaders move beyond a command-and-control mindset, they actually position others around them to be more flexible in the face of change—whether change happens organizationally, or at the product level. This shift can unlock a much larger strategic advantage.

As Cable asserts, there are two main strategic advantages that come with this type of shift. "First, organizations begin to move toward proactive innovation," he says. This happens when everyone possesses a shared understanding of real purpose, in real time. "The message becomes, 'I can make decisions to do things in a new way, and I'm not waiting for your authority. I already have the authority, because I know what *we're* trying to accomplish.'"

This is a powerful link in the larger story of innovation— one we'll return to in Part Two, when we take a deeper look at failure. Here, the idea of trying new things doesn't come from a 'fail fast/fail often' mindset, but rather one that emanates from individual purpose. The person behind the idea feels pre-vetted to think in new ways. They've been empowered to bring their best thought to the table, and it aligns with the shared vision.

"The very idea of fast innovation depends on working from a shared purpose," Cable says. "You can think of the shared purpose, or the shared mechanism of purpose, as its own sort of control. It creates alignment through coordinated and coherent action." Purpose-shared innovation starts with a very essential precept: no leader has all of the answers. Cable encourages people to drive things forward in order to find answers, as do many other leaders who see alignment as a path toward innovation.

The second strategic advantage to alignment points directly to a number of business intangibles, such as energy, enthusiasm, and resilience. In short, alignment literally energizes people. As Cable says, "This goes back to physiology and brain chemistry. When people know they can try new things as part of a shared, vetted, and purpose-driven framework, they play from their strengths. They push forward in personal and meaningful ways." In such an environment, people are enthusiastic, curious, and engaged with their work. They are eager to be part of the solution, and to take on new challenges as they come.

Organizations that embrace digital product transformation, and adopt practices like lean or agile management, need alignment in order to gain a deeper understanding of what great strategy looks like, and see the link between insights, planning, management, focus, and outcomes. Through alignment, organizations create conditions and circumstances that put them in position to find market fit, navigate the complexity of product and development life cycles, and operationalize toward success. If achieved, alignment becomes an organization's most significant competitive advantage when they seek to deliver digital products and services.

Alignment also spurs a learning mindset that propels organizations forward. As a competitive advantage, it has the power to drive revenue, increase the quality of products and services, and create new operational efficiencies. If leaders are responsible for empowering their people, then they must be the ones who unlock key areas of critical thinking that either breed success, or, when missed, lead to failure.

In Part Two, we'll take a deeper look at why failure happens, and how alignment can be the key to avoiding it.

PART TWO
SIGNS OF MISALIGNMENT

Beyond the market: internal sabotage

Root causes of misalignment and failure

- Not knowing your users or customers
- Mismanaging expectations
- Underestimating organizational complexity and scale
- Ignoring accumulated or inherited debt
- Overlooking the cost of siloed knowledge
- Skipping steps
- Misdirecting capabilities and resources
- Lacking a shared understanding

A first-hand account of failure

Evidence & impacts of failure

Symptomatic issues & impact chart

Learning from failure

PART TWO

Signs of Misalignment

"Often, the introduction of any new technology, whether digital or not, fails because of an assumption that comes from a *Field of Dreams* mentality: 'If you build it, they will come.' What you're doing is introducing a new thing into a complex system. This forces you to think about the rest of the system, and the ripple effect that comes with introducing the new thing. People need to explore the problems broadly enough to understand what it will take for a new product to successfully meet expectations, whatever those expectations are."

– Deborah Mrazek, founding partner, Curiate

When you introduce a new digital product into a complex ecosystem, you must think about the dozens, even hundreds of facets that exist within that system, along with changes the new product will bring. This critical consideration stands at the trailhead of every initiative. Ignoring it is the first step toward failure.

In order to discuss failure, it's important to consider what's happening inside the leadership suites of many organizations. Are leaders exploring potential problems through broad-enough lenses? Do they understand what it takes for new products to meet the expectations of customers/users, and match desired outcomes? Are they equipped to address expectations and outcomes, whether positive or negative?

BEYOND THE MARKET: INTERNAL SABOTAGE

When I began looking at why so many digital products and transformation initiatives fail, a lack of market fit tended to be the main reason. It seemed like a simple equation: if a product doesn't meet the needs of users, it won't succeed. However, what I've discovered over time is that the lack of market fit doesn't necessarily cause failure, but is often the *result* of other failures that happen earlier in the process. In most cases, these earlier failures go overlooked, or are completely ignored. Quite often, leaders and teams literally skip some fairly fundamental steps. For instance:

- They don't identify their core customer, or make the distinction between buyers and users.
- They don't take into account the deeper contextual environment involved in addressing alternative options, or the cost burden of switching to a new product.

When leaders ignore chronic internal breakdowns, they prevent organizations from connecting with customers, gathering actionable insights, and working through the process to establish market fit. In so doing, they sabotage their organizations.

Quite often, something else is at play as well. In many cases, product initiatives that will eventually fail get off to solid starts. After all, even highly dysfunctional organizations can overcome certain problems if a product finds an early market fit. We can all think of cases where someone introduces the right product at the right time, and enjoys a boom that might last a few quarters. Strong early returns can make it easy to forget about lingering issues. The bad news is that a strong market fit will only take you so far on its own. If you ignore the holes in key areas such as customer experience and operations, you'll eventually sink.

This brings up the issue of ego, and its relationship with misunderstanding the meaning of 'fail fast/fail often,' which I mentioned in Part One.

"Plenty of case studies show why failure happens," says Tatyana Mamut, CPO of Nextdoor, a social networking service that focuses on neighborhood vitality and connections. "However, the root cause often points back to bad leaders with big egos."

In a transformation environment, a good leader needs to understand that what they've done in the past is not always going to produce success going forward. "As a leader, you need to step back, understand the goals, and put your agenda aside," Mamut contends. "When you put your habits into question, you can figure out what an organization needs, and how to adapt, so initiatives go in the right direction."

I'm sure we've all been in meetings where someone frames the concept of failure as a positive. In certain environments, failure means being bold, taking risks, and trying to move the ball downfield. It's a sign of fearlessness, driven by the urge to disrupt the status quo. I understand the lure of this mindset, and have certainly been in those meetings. However, the 'fail fast/fail often' mantra can be dangerous, even toxic, when it does not align with what consumers/users want and need, ignores the importance of behavioral data, or pushes too hard against an organization's culture.

Let's look at some hard facts that help balance things out. According to the International Data Corporation (IDC), global spending on digital transformation will approach $2 trillion by 2022.[8] When you consider the high likelihood of failure, that's hundreds of billions of dollars in losses. In addition, the compounding effects of failure translate to more debt, lost jobs, and shuttered businesses. In this reality, leaders cannot afford to misunderstand the meaning of 'fail fast/fail often.'

Granted, a culture that is proud of its willingness to fail might entice job candidates, and get people excited about working in a bold, risk-taking environment. It's easy to celebrate the person with the big idea, and even revel in stories of the failures they encounter along the way. However, a true understanding of their journey tends to get lost in the applause. Without experimentation and incremental delivery, 'fail fast/fail often' can crash under the weight of lofty expectations, especially within the context of digital product transformation. It should never be the singular mantra that guides product teams forward.

A cardinal sin in the world of digital product transformation is to build business cases based on big ideas and unvalidated assumptions. The sad thing is, at this moment, someone who possesses organizational authority is trying to do just that. When all is said and done, they are most likely going to fail.

When someone blindly trusts assumptions, or decides that their big idea is reason enough, they're taking their organization down a dangerous path. People who trust assumptions, but won't do the legwork to validate them, can be dangerous, especially if they're in leadership positions. It suggests a command-and-control leadership style that emanates from 'my way or the highway' arrogance. While there are plenty of cases where people don't know what they don't know, ignorance should never be an excuse for failure. Instead, leaders and their teams must go looking for answers that address customer and user needs, and then work from this understanding as they seek alignment at the four levels from Part One (Individual, Team, Organizational, and Market).

ROOT CAUSES OF MISALIGNMENT AND FAILURE

"People have confirmation bias. They look at things to confirm their beliefs, but don't look for what's causing problems, or seek insight."

– Indi Young, founding partner, Adaptive Path

The vast majority of companies—as high as 89%—have either adopted a digital-first business strategy, or plan to do so in the near future.[9] They understand that digital product transformation will improve the customer experience, create or expand operational models, and spur new efficiencies. As you can imagine, this awareness can generate a great deal of internal pressure, and force many leaders into false comfort zones where their egos take control. Instead of getting to know the unknown, they tell their troops to charge forward. Think of someone you know who has a big ego. Do they always need to be right? How often do they over-commit, or make promises they can't keep? Do they need praise, or try to change rules when the current ones don't work for them?

To navigate change, build high-performance teams, and deliver successful digital products, a leader's ego must be checked. Otherwise, an ego-first leadership style will damage relationships, demoralize subordinates and colleagues, and subjugate team-minded attributes such as empathy, collaboration, and informed decision making. Egocentric leaders are putting their own agendas first, and literally working against the very principles of alignment.

Through research, interviews, and my professional experience, I have identified eight of the most common causes of misalignment, and listed them below. When an unchecked ego permeates through a digital product initiative, it can exacerbate every one of them.

1. NOT KNOWING YOUR USERS OR CUSTOMERS

"Organizations often see research or customer experience as more of a point of validation, versus trying to understand something deeper within their user or customer base."

– Christie McAllister, experience research manager, digital platform experience, Autodesk

When companies say they're user-centric, but don't engage with users, no one wins. However, when they operate in a way that embraces user-centric principles, they create value for those who rely on their products or services.

Misalignment between what it means to be user-centric, and how it looks in practice, can lead to catastrophic results. At the core, you'll find a lack of empathy for the user, plus plenty of bias and assumptions coming from leadership, and/or the product team. The impacts can be seen in a number of bottom line drivers, such as:

- Weak market position relative to competitors
- Higher user acquisition cost
- Decreased product or service adoption

- Higher cost of ownership
- More customer complaints
- High attrition rate/churn rate
- Weak customer loyalty
- Unsustainable operating costs

There are also situations when leaders simply don't understand—or don't care to understand—the difference between users and customers. Recognizing the distinction between who *uses* your product, and who *pays for it* is vital. Ignoring it will lead to misalignment that shows up in key stages and the supporting user flows across a customer's journey, including:

- Awareness
- Consideration
- Commitment (a.k.a. purchase)
- Adopt and serve
- Retain
- Expand

2. MISMANAGING EXPECTATIONS

BALANCING REALISTIC EXPECTATIONS

"Expectations are a form of first-class truth: If people believe it, it's true."

– Bill Gates, co-founder, Microsoft

The way you handle expectations can be the difference between success and failure. Without clear expectations, you compromise efforts, erode trust, and put the success of your product team at risk. Worse, when you set unreasonable expectations, you may inadvertently force teams to skip steps in order to hit unrealistic deadlines.

Consider some of the projects you've worked on. How much time did leaders spend trying to articulate and explain the vision, or the value of the product or service? Did they communicate the vision the same way each time? Perhaps the message changed with different audiences, leaving teams uncertain about goals, aspirations, and opportunities involved. Did everyone possess a clear understanding of the problems that the initiative was meant to solve? Were the right people on board? How well did team leaders manage expectations across the organization, from the C-suite, down to the product team level?

3. UNDERESTIMATING ORGANIZATIONAL COMPLEXITY AND SCALE

"The single biggest problem in communication is
the illusion that it has taken place."

– George Bernard Shaw, playwright and critic

As projects grow and teams scale, maintaining effective communication becomes more complicated—and this complexity can be a significant blind spot. As teams become larger, the gap between decision makers and customers/users grows.

Leaders and teams must be able to clearly communicate the digital product's strategic foundation. When two people work closely together, the communication follows a back-and-forth line. When you add a handful of people, things begin to triangulate. By the time you get a dozen or more people involved, you can wind up creating splinters and silos in a misaligned environment.

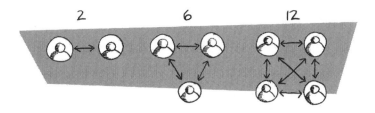

"How many different versions of the truth are out there," is how Chris Cravens, founding CIO of Uber and Zynga, puts it. "Different versions of the truth mean different expected outcomes. When that's the case, how can a team align with one ultimate purpose?"

Priorities steer teams toward accomplishing outcomes, while measures tell people when they've arrived. Without a clear framework, and effective communication—which includes documenting priorities, outcomes, and measures—people and groups will go their own way. When this happens, teams will never deliver exceptional value.

4. IGNORING ACCUMULATED OR INHERITED DEBT

DIGITAL PRODUCT EVOLUTION

"You have to make sure to address tech and design debt, so things don't crumble. If you let issues grow, they're only going to slow you down going forward."

– Katherine Nester, CPO, Ruby Receptionists

Debt comes in many forms, and each type will impact a product's success in different ways. Technical and design debt are two of the most common types that show up in digital product transformations. Whether you accumulate or inherit one or both, it's essential to manage them.

Technical debt is a concept that many digital professionals and leaders are familiar with. Coined by Ward Cunningham in the early 1990s, it often accrues because one or more of the following are substandard:

- Software architecture
- Source code
- Development practices
- Modularity
- Code complexity and interoperability management
- Knowledge management and documentation
- Planning for depreciated technology

Maybe the code was poorly written at the start. Perhaps, in an effort to cut costs and save time, the product team designed and developed for short-term gains, without considering future implications. Whatever the case may be, any technical debt you inherit or incur will accrue interest as time goes by. You will be forced to pay it down in money, lost time, and resources. Eventually, you will either have to go backwards and refactor, consolidate, or completely rewrite part or all of your digital product.

Design debt occurs because of poor design choices. For instance, you create UX concepts or solutions to reach short-term goals, instead of focusing on a design system that can adapt to changes in product architecture, flows, interactions, and visual language. As an example, rather than thinking about scalability, you simply add elements until you create mounds of clutter that make your product unusable.

Design debt will continue to accrue for a number of reasons. For instance:

- Your product design lacks a grounded strategy.
- You need insights and/or context to guide decisions.
- You focus on aesthetics, rather than user outcomes.
- You lack documentation of design decisions.
- You do not put a style guide or design system in place to manage fragmentation.

Companies pay steep prices when they overlook the importance of user-centric design. If they unintentionally create something that becomes an unwieldly or otherwise disposable digital product, customers will eventually lose interest.

5. OVERLOOKING THE COST OF SILOED KNOWLEDGE

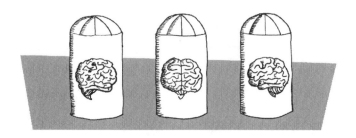

"As a leader, you want to equip teams with clarity, so everyone understands, in no uncertain terms, what's happening, and why. One test is to see if people can repeat essential information back to you in a very short exchange, like an elevator pitch. That way, if a leader asks someone what the project is about, they'll be able to answer by citing what the organization is trying to accomplish, and break things down by steps over time."

— Chris Cravens, founding CIO of Uber and Zynga

Siloed knowledge creates tremendous barriers to success. Unfortunately, very few organizations possess the type of knowledge management that enables teams to work together seamlessly, and communicate upstream and down. Instead, critical institutional knowledge is locked away, hoarded by key people, and split into fragments. Previous decisions remain unclear, and accessibility to essential information is limited. When siloed knowledge is the norm, an organization will not be able to do any of the following easily:

- Act quickly to take advantage of new business opportunities.
- Identify interdependencies to solve a problem effectively.
- Mitigate design or technical debt.
- Meet budgets and timelines with available resources, while effectively managing expectations.
- Reach critical velocity, which can significantly impact performance and outcomes.

When critical information is locked away in silos, people wind up spending more time in meetings, starting and stopping work, revalidating user and business requirements, and creating additional rework deliverables. All too often, organizations accept this reality because they feel like it actually saves them time, somehow reduces costs, or makes it easier for members of workgroups to put their heads down and plow forward. Unfortunately, this shortsighted approach will eventually create more costs, and increase long-term organizational debt.

Conversely, when leaders and teams have access to a rich source of critical knowledge, they are equipped to identify and understand the following:

- Context (what the product is, and what challenge it will solve)
- Intended outcomes (for users by type and scenario)
- Business rules (an explanation of why things matter)
- User flows and stories
- Technology ecosystems
- Business interdependencies
- Functional requirements

6. SKIPPING STEPS

"Basically, you can't skip steps. You have to put one foot in front of the other. Things take time. There are no shortcuts. But you want to do those steps with passion and ferocity."

– Jeff Bezos, founder and CEO, Amazon

Skipping steps is a great way to fall on your face. It happens when leaders prioritize moving faster, getting things done cheaper, and rushing to respond to the next big craze. In the short term, it can look like you're being hyper-efficient. Maybe you cut timelines down, or create a larger feature set in a hurry. However, when you skip steps in order to speed up a release, you risk reducing your ROI, and even derail the product.

In some cases, organizations knowingly skip steps that they don't think are important within the product development life cycle. Other times, they recognize the importance of a step, but can't articulate what success looks like. Rather than go deeper into the step, they graze the surface, then move along.

The fact is, every step involved in creating a great product exists for a reason. Meanwhile, every discipline includes its own set of steps toward solving problems, and operationalizing solutions. I'll come back to a number of key steps in Part Four. For now, the main takeaway is that skipping steps will not breed success.

7. MISDIRECTING CAPABILITIES AND RESOURCES

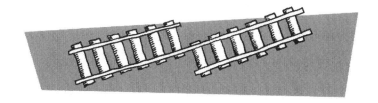

"The groundwork needs to happen at the very beginning. It saves time. It saves arguments. It saves you from a lot of wasted effort."

– Lindsay Main, head of trade marketing, adidas

A plan without a clear strategy is worthless, and perhaps even dangerous. It gives people a false sense of clarity and security, which can lead to failure. When companies focus on planning without a strategy, they often misalign the capabilities and resources they need to achieve success.

Parts Three and Four will focus a great deal on the relationship and the differences between planning and strategy. To start the conversation now, it's important to know that a plan can offer a quick fix, but won't help unravel the complexities that await. While a plan may help you take a first step, without a strategy, you will not be able to maintain momentum. In the end, a plan without a strategy will lead to failure, because most plans lack the following:

- A solid strategic foundation
- Adaptability
- Focus on outcomes
- Clarity of the challenges, interdependencies and prerequisites for success
- Transparency
- An understanding of available resources

Strategies, on the other hand, include tactics that define exactly what you're going to do, how you'll execute, and what comes next. A strategy helps to account for unknowns, prepare for changes, prioritize resources, and build a framework for critical decision making. When you follow a strategy, you put teams on the path to success.

8. LACKING A SHARED UNDERSTANDING

"Without a shared understanding, you're missing critical context for asking better questions, making better and more informed decisions, and having the right checks and balances in the process."

– Jared Spool, founding principal, User Interface Engineering

The path toward a shared understanding starts with possessing a common language. Within the context of this book, the phrase 'common language' refers to a collective awareness of how and why things happen, and the ability to discuss every point in between. Think of a common language as being the internal 'rules of the game.' Teams and individuals must understand, acknowledge, and work within the framework of a common language if an organization wants to foster a shared understanding, and build a strategic foundation that everyone agrees on.

The need for a common language and shared understanding amplifies as a company evolves. If people within the organization can't understand each other, how will the organization adopt, integrate, and leverage their digital products and services? When everyone interprets things differently, you cannot communicate effectively. The disconnect can lead to frustration, confusion, and distrust at every level. In an environment that lacks a shared understanding of what's happening and why, you'll hear teams and workers make comments like these:

- "They have no idea what they're talking about."
- "Do they know what they're doing?"
- "Why do we keep going over this?"
- "This is never going to happen."

When people can't communicate, their lack of a shared understanding will drag down the group's collective competency, regardless of how much talent an organization possesses.

A FIRST-HAND ACCOUNT OF FAILURE

In Part One, I shared a first-hand account of a large project that moved with alignment from start to finish. Now it's time for a different story.

I mentioned strategic foundation above, and will come back to it a few more times throughout the book. Possessing a strategic foundation is vital if you want your digital product transformation to succeed. It's also something that many leaders misunderstand. It's important to know that, no matter how strong your strategic foundation is, if you don't communicate it clearly—and if people don't accept it broadly across your organization—your digital product transformation cannot achieve alignment.

Years ago, I was on a team that came in midstream to work on a substantial global project for a leading manufacturer. The project we entered was severely misaligned, but we were able to get it on course, and minimize the client's losses. They invited us to lead the next two iterations of their digital platform, and we exceeded their expectations both times. However, when we returned for yet another iteration, things did not go so well.

For starters, the project scope had ballooned. Plus, there were dozens of new stakeholders, and the internal management structure was completely splintered. In addition, no one agreed on a shared vision, or an established strategic foundation. People argued about the platform, and as internal teams tried to hash things out, the clock kept ticking toward launch. Feeling rushed, people started to skip steps. No one vetted any of the feedback or direction they shared with us, in part because no internal team took ownership of the strategic process. Instead, groups focused only on their own priorities, often through the lens of siloed interpretations and goals. There was no accountability, and absolutely no alignment.

Any time multiple groups and partners come together, different interpretations can happen. That's why it's essential for people and teams to align around a single strategic foundation that reinforces the reason why every step matters. Otherwise, management systems fall apart, motivations dim, and attitudes sour. When workgroups only focus on their self-preservation, they will eventually throw other groups under the bus—which is where we wound up at the end. By the time the project was wrapping up, more than 80 people on the client's side were working on it—double the number from the previous year. Meanwhile, their $500,000 budget had become $2M in projected costs. They were essentially throwing money at a problem that was irreconcilable due to their constraints.

As I revisit this anecdote, it's easy to track nearly every cause of misalignment I shared in the previous section:

- Project leaders lost sight of users and customers.
- The internal structure made it impossible to manage expectations.
- Inherited debt festered.
- Teams retreated into silos in order to protect themselves.
- No one owned the strategic foundation, causing confusion.
- Without the foundation, it was impossible to align capabilities and resources.
- As organizational complexity and scale ballooned, no one was accountable to communicating what was happening, or ensuring that everyone understood why.

Understanding the *what* and *why* of any project is vital. Sadly, the above scenario isn't unique. Countless organizations lose sight of what it takes to succeed at a digital product transformation—even those that have previously been successful. We can explore the *what* in a number of ways. For instance:

- What does change mean at the leadership level?
- What will change mean to managers and employees?
- What does the product transformation need to achieve?
- What will it take to realize intended outcomes?
- What measurements will the organization use to track progress and evaluate success?

Addressing questions like these can give teams a new level of strategic clarity, and help leaders focus on the right things. In addition, when organizations prioritize the following foundational layers, they can anticipate potential stumbling blocks, and build steps that will lead to success:

- What does the organization need?
- What's happening internally (controllable factors)?
- What's happening externally (uncontrollable factors)?

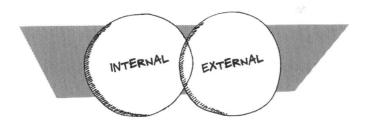

In the story above, the market did not derail the initiative. Instead, a series of internal factors at multiple operational levels created severe, untenable misalignment—conditions which made it impossible to achieve success.

EVIDENCE & IMPACTS OF MISALIGNMENT

Why does failure happen at such a large scale? Shouldn't organizations and leaders know better? Many do. However, the vast majority of digital product transformations fail because leaders do not possess a reference that shows them what success looks like. Whether it's through a lack of experiential wisdom, or having not studied initiatives from outside of the organization, this misunderstanding can create a number of pitfalls, and impact an organization for years to come.

No matter why failure happens—a big ego, bad timing, poor response to pressure, market fatigue, tech debt, etc.— you can often spot evidence of misalignment along the way. To do so, you have to be willing to look for it, and able to recognize it for what it is. You can also measure the impacts of various missteps, or moments of misalignment, as demonstrated in the chart that follows:

SYMPTOMATIC ISSUES & IMPACT CHART

Misalignment	Possible Evidence	Common Impacts
• Poor or incomplete product strategy and definition of the right solution	• No clear companywide focus and strategy • Weak product vision • Poorly defined user needs/problem • Poorly defined outcomes • Poorly defined business requirements • Undefined interdependencies • No product plan/roadmap • No investment strategy • Lack of data to fuel decision making • Misalignment internally (conflict)	• Cost overruns • Time delays • Expectations management • High risk of missing short-term and long-term outcomes • Missed revenue or cost reduction opportunities • Inadequate resources
• Weak product delivery and performance	• Lack of stakeholder buy-in and/or involvement • Ineffective or incomplete planning • Undefined business KPIs • Lack of user insight and/or participation • Undocumented friction points (users/employees)	• Cost overruns • Time delays • Expectations management • Missed product delivery • Design debt • Technical debt • Quality control issues • Product/service performance issues

	• Unclear or inconsistent customer/user experience • Undefined user KPIs • Lack of internal capacity and/or knowledge • Undefined expertise, roles and responsibilities • Siloed strategy, design and engineering disciplines • Under resourced • Product/service complexity • No functional requirements documentation • Poor information architecture • Poor visual design & interactions • Poor data architecture • Undocumented or practiced software-development governance policies • Poor product/ service differentiation • No continuous delivery (product optimization)	• Product compatibility issues • Product maintainability issues • Product scalability issues • Reduced Consumer confidence and satisfaction • Poor customer feedback and reviews • Increased cost per customer/user acquisition • Lower or failed customer/user adoption • Lower active customer/user frequency rate • Decreased lifetime customer/user value • Lower customer/ user retention rate • Increased customer/user level of effort (LOE) • Increased employee/user level of effort • Decreased employee satisfaction • Internal stakeholders will not approve next phases • Increasingly vulnerable to competition

Imagine how frustrating it is to work in a highly coordinated way, yet still fail. Maybe you don't have to imagine it. Maybe you've experienced it. Was it because of missteps? Willful ignorance? Ego? Without experience, or the level of understanding that leaders gain through research and discovery, it can be impossible to know what steps you need to hit, or why they matter. Even when people are clear about an idea, they may still fall under the spell of a false sense of security. The truth is, it's easy to embrace the attitude that says a great idea is all you need. Unfortunately, product transformations require more than a great idea if they're going to succeed—especially when leaders don't comprehend or appreciate the complexities involved. No one can expect leaders to understand *everything* that goes into a successful digital product transformation. However, leaders must be able to build and communicate the strategy, and establish the right environment that will empower a team to deliver a great product experience.

LEARNING FROM FAILURE

"The greatest teacher, failure is."

– Yoda, Jedi Master

No one wants to fail. In most scenarios, 'failure' is a bad word. Most people don't want to talk about failure before, during, or after the fact. It can be painful, messy, and embarrassing. It can end careers and relationships. For a business, it can mean lost opportunities, devastating cost overruns, wasted time, and much worse.

The thing is, failure is something everyone can learn from. When you understand failure, you can navigate it, adapt to it, and pivot when the time comes. In fact, when you let failure be a teacher, you and your teams can begin to perform better, which will create a strategic advantage for your organization.

Failure doesn't happen by accident. It's the result of misalignment. In order to achieve alignment, it helps to understand how and why failure happens. You may grimace at the idea of hundreds of billions of dollars dedicated to failed projects, but you still have to look failure in the eye. The figures are ugly, but they're also preventable. If you want to prevent these types of losses, you must get acquainted with failure.

I'd like you to consider two questions that relate to the health and viability of your organization, and any digital product transformation initiatives you're facing:

1. Can everyone, from the C-suite down through the product team, clearly communicate how the organization's vision dovetails with the product's strategy?
2. Can you identify areas where you may be misaligned, in order to name the risks you face?

These questions are just starting points. To answer them, I invite you to retrace the steps of a previous failure, as I did in my earlier example. When you do, what you'll find is, at some point, the initiative became misaligned, yet people and teams kept going forward.

When you're misaligned, it's impossible to create and move forward with an effective strategic foundation. Meanwhile, without a clear vision of the future, nothing will hold people or groups together, or encourage teams to be accountable.

Catching and calling out misalignment can be a tall order, especially if the concept of doing so is new. To help, you must examine and attend to each mission-critical step along the way. Often, this includes the following:

- Constructing multidisciplinary teams composed of individuals who care.
- Building and agreeing on a strategic foundation that aligns with the company's purpose.
- Addressing an actual need that generates enough value.
- Ensuring that your product is integrated into your culture, while staying true to the needs of customers/users.

These concerns possess measurable impacts on your organization. As the process continues, your questions may trend in the following directions:

- What's the scope of design or technical debt?
- Does the product/service have performance or compatibility issues?
- What quality control issues are you dealing with?
- How easily can you maintain it?
- Does it scale?
- Is your audience (whether consumers or internal teams) going to use this product/service with confidence?

Ultimately, a digital product transformation that achieves and maintains alignment will cost a fraction of what you'll spend on a misaligned initiative. Your product will be stronger when it goes to market, and will achieve your goals while providing the benefits that users seek. On the other end of the spectrum, you can trace a weak product and service delivery all the way back to not having answered, then re-answered the following questions:

- Why are we doing this?
- What do we wish to accomplish?

What does it take to get leaders to ask and answer these questions? How do leaders make sure their answers extend clearly to every member of the product team? In Part Three, we'll focus on leading with alignment.

PART THREE
LEADING WITH ALIGNMENT

Think differently: beyond the product—platforms
- Platforms defined
- The platform era: contrast of expectations and impact

Beyond the business model: experience, application, and data
- Experience
- Application
- Data

Servant leadership
- Optimism vs. expectations
- Truth vs. reality

The necessity of being trilingual: business + design + technology

Focus on the right things at the right time

Revisit your relationship with data: transactional vs. behavioral

Planning is not strategy
- Planning through a leadership lens
- Strategy through a leadership lens

Aligning strategy & execution

PART THREE
Leading with Alignment

"A leader's job, wherever you are in the chain of command, is to tell people what the future looks like. It starts with a vision, and leads to an outcome. Your message must be, 'When we're done, X will look like this.' And, you must do so in clear, concrete terms. You want to give people something they can anchor to. If you don't, they will find something on their own. You have to break things down at a micro level, and make your descriptions clear to the point where team members know what has to happen at every phase."

– Chris Cravens, founding CIO of Uber and Zynga

To be a leader of digital products and services in today's world, you need to possess a brand-new set of knowledge and skills. Throughout Part Three, I'd like to focus on key leadership concepts that will help you build alignment, create powerful strategies, lead teams through the product development life cycle, and succeed.

To start, let's explore the difference between creating one-off products, and building platforms that adapt and scale over time. After all, this is the landscape in which you must lead with alignment.

THINK DIFFERENTLY: BEYOND THE PRODUCT—PLATFORMS

What does it mean to build a product that is a platform? To a large degree, it involves building something that will extend beyond itself as it goes into the world. However, that definition seems a little vague. Building what, exactly? A technology? A car? A new kind of running shoe?

Previous ideology promoted building stand-alone, monolithic solutions. Platforms, on the other hand, enable increased precision, performance, modularity, and dependability to align with the needs of users—and with the expectations of the market. In today's digital landscape, leaders must understand the larger story of platforms, and not just what they mean through the lens of a business model framework.

PLATFORMS DEFINED

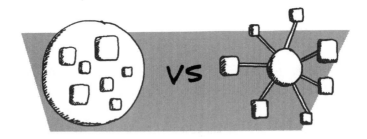

Platforms are designed to adapt in an era of rampant change. They enable growth and scale, amplify the value of your offering, and go beyond the problem you're solving. They provide a foundational architecture for new capabilities and efficiencies, and strengthen the connections between processes, systems, and data sources.

David Rogers presents a concise definition in his work, *The Digital Transformation Playbook*. As he writes, a platform in tech "may be any underlying software on which additional programs are built."[10] In that way, platforms create the ability to build new capabilities and touchpoints, and improve tools and processes.

Platforms are everywhere. We see them in media, marketing, shopping, entertainment, gaming, hospitality, medicine, and many other industries and facets of life. They bring people and services together: drivers and riders; vacationers and homeowners with a spare room; content creators, consumers, and advertisers. Whether it's Amazon Web Services (AWS), Airbnb, which Rogers mentions in his book, eBay, Etsy, Spotify, Lyft, Netflix, Uber, or YouTube, most platforms function with a similar set of parameters that involve the following:

- Producers (content, products, and services)
- Consumers (buyers and/or users, and developers)
- Technology (the connection point)

It's important to note that not all platforms are two-sided markets. There are many technology platforms, including AWS, Microsoft Azure, IBM Watson, Splunk and others, that enable digital products, but are invisible to the end user.

As you explore platform-related experiences, a more complete definition of a platform comes to the surface. You begin to see a platform as a service or solution that extends beyond the simplicity of being a one-off tool, and sets a foundational architecture for scalability, flexibility, and evolution in order to stay relevant.

For example, YouTube is not a product—it's a virtual staging ground for news, stories, music, and curated experiences. Some people profit because of YouTube. Others use it as a way to build audiences, communicate their opinions, and connect. A platform doesn't seek to get customers to use *it*. Instead, a platform focuses on building a world that connects customers and providers, or, in many cases, customers and customers. When you see how Airbnb, or eBay, or any number of platforms operate, you discover that they create a pivot that generates revenue on both sides of the relationship.

Here's an overview to help guide your thinking about building platforms, in comparison to monolithic models of one-off digital products:

- At a very basic level, traditional products that are not platforms do not adapt well, if at all. They cannot sustain disruption. On the other hand, platforms align with broader thinking, and can respond nimbly in disruptive times.
- When you invest in, and align with platform thinking, you put your organization in a position to continue influencing the market and users over the long term.
- A platform-minded approach is aware of obsolescence. Any platform-based product becomes a component in a much larger ecosystem. On one hand, it fulfills a need; on the other, it opens doors that extend to new possibilities.
- In certain situations, platforms may require more initial upfront effort to build, but they can accelerate the path toward growth and change.
- Additionally, platforms are far more adaptable over time. Ultimately, investing more time at the beginning pays dividends in the end.

- Within any platform, there will typically be a series of features built one on top of the other. Each feature brings its own value, but only exists because the platform allows it to.

- Through a platform approach, an organization can scale its thinking and strategic decisions to shift when opportunities arise, building other solutions that are adjacent, yet different enough from one another. A platform-minded product expands laterally as a whole, while smaller feature sets can move vertically.

- Working from platform-focused thinking, leaders can utilize value from other parts of the organization, and/or from external partners. This adds an extra layer of lateral movement to the equation, and builds the ecosystem out even wider.

It's important to note that when you're creating or transforming a digital product, you have to know how it aligns with your company's strategic objectives. You need to understand the problem it solves, how it benefits users, and how it will potentially move your organization forward. I'll put more emphasis on these topics in Part Four. For now, one key point to keep in mind is that, when you're creating something new, or transforming an existing product, you may be dealing with an underlying sense of urgency. This can instigate a 'strike while the iron is hot' mindset. When you realize the inherent potential of platform thinking, your mindset becomes more customer-focused. You know what your customers need today, and you keep an eye on how the solution fits into the future.

This approach leads to a deeper understanding and awareness of key dimensions you might be overlooking. Working from a platform mindset can prompt essential questions, and help teams make informed decisions. This will ensure that during every phase of the process—from developing your strategic vision, all the way through the product development life cycle and support—you'll find checks and balances that guide your thinking, support your people, and help your processes maintain alignment.

THE PLATFORM ERA: CONTRAST OF EXPECTATIONS AND IMPACT

When companies launch a digital product, they often want to create a new experience, or automate and/or re-energize an existing one. For example, a company might introduce a solution that lets users find and sell products online. (This may not sound revolutionary today, but 20 years ago, plenty of people were asking, 'What's eBay all about?') The point isn't the past, but the future. What happens when the next great disruptive solution comes along and displaces the way things currently work?

Designing and launching a product from a platform mindset is a hedge against the inevitability of competition, displacement, and the rapid pace of change. There are hundreds, perhaps thousands of examples of companies that have seen an eager and excited consumer base quickly adopt disruptive, platform-minded products (think of the iPhone, or Netflix). Now, think about the products and business models that had been market leaders before these platforms replaced them. Perhaps you still have a flip phone in a drawer in your house. You can dig it out for a road trip to the country's last Blockbuster store in the middle of Oregon.

How did we arrive in the era of platforms? In many ways, advances in mobile technology, connectivity, and the ability to manage large amounts of data have conspired to get us here.

However, these capabilities are only part of the equation. Consumer demand, desire, and expectations play roles as well.

Amara's Law, attributed to Roy Amara, an American researcher and futurist, comes to mind when I think about the way that people place expectations on technology. As Amara's Law states, "We tend to overestimate the effect of a technology in the short run, and underestimate the effect in the long run."[11] A graphical illustration of Amara's Law looks like this:

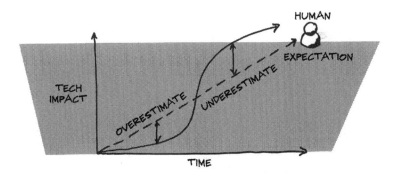

When we overlay Amara's Law with the notion of platform thinking, we gain a sense of how expectations drive product development and execution. For example, prior to Uber, very few people envisioned Uber. After Uber, everything *must* work like Uber. Eventually, the market levels off, and the business model that was fresh and new a decade ago becomes the status quo. It happens repeatedly. Soon, the next disrupter will find its way into the market, and Amara's S-curve will push toward a new rise.

Let's step back for a moment, and consider the internet itself. Steve Case, former CEO of AOL, illustrated this in his reference to three distinct phases of the internet:[12]

- Phase 1.0 was all about building the necessary infrastructure. Hardware makers thrived.
- Phase 2.0 brought the launch of businesses and business models that could only exist *because* of the internet. Without the web, how would we 'google' a restaurant, 'instagram' a picture, or 'netflix' a movie? (It's amazing how quickly some brand names become transitive verbs.)
- Phase 3.0 is where we find ourselves today. The internet is linked to how we work, live, and play. It's on our desks, inside the walls of smart houses, in our pockets, and on our wrists. We rely on it every time we tap an app to check the weather, schedule a ride, or take advantage of two-day delivery guarantee.

Our current phase is a precursor to a much larger digital transformation taking place on a global scale, thanks in part to the increased adoption of the Internet of Things (IoT). Ubiquitous connectivity will continue to pave the way for greater innovation and automation—and revolutionize people's expectations. Organizations need to enhance their business models now if they want to create value, and stay viable in this new era.

Countless tools and services that already exist serve as enablers that allow innovation to happen faster, and at a greater scale than anything we've seen before. This coincides with an increased rate of adoption, as eager consumers and users are ready to up-level as soon as new tools hit the market. Right now, the digital landscape is rapidly shifting due to the following:

- Computation cycles are becoming faster.
- Storage capabilities are getting larger, cheaper, and more secure, while coming in smaller form factors.
- More connected devices are making it into homes, cars, workplaces, and pockets across the globe.
- Geolocation, tagging, and GPS have become product norms.
- Instant connectivity is moving toward ubiquity.
- AI, machine learning, and machine autonomy are unlocking new possibilities.
- Automation is taking humans out of the equation of many tasks.

Every day, we tap into tools and capabilities that seem to have come from the future. They create new market possibilities, drive consumer desires, and reconfigure expectations. We grow accustomed to things being simpler, faster, less expensive, and more efficient. We know that, at any hour, any day, there's a digital platform doing one of the following three things:

- Assisting someone in the moment, typically by simplifying or automating some of the work.
- Augmenting something by adding to it, thereby increasing its value.
- Amplifying someone's experience of a product by enhancing its performance.

Chances are, there are apps on your phone right now that will let you order food, host a video call, buy a stock, or move money between bank accounts. As more applications and solutions emerge, consumer demands and expectations will reach new levels. Do we know what's coming next? Can we anticipate the ways that change will move us forward? With so much occurring, the old model of just dropping a product into the market will not suffice. Organizations need to find areas of opportunity to create value, solve challenges, eliminate inconveniences, and increase their own relevance. Via digital product transformation, they can change the game, and deliver on promises and goals. Still, many leaders struggle to grasp the full scope of what digital product transformation is, and how to effectively drive strategy, define solutions, and bridge the execution gap. They're not up to speed when it comes to adapting business models, improving operations, spurring a competitive advantage, and enhancing the customer experience.

BEYOND THE BUSINESS MODEL: EXPERIENCE, APPLICATION, AND DATA

No matter what digital product transformation looks like for your organization, it is essential if you want to keep from going extinct. Saying *yes* to it can involve many things, including:

- Creating something new
- Augmenting existing offerings
- Modernizing
- Improving workflows
- Optimizing processes
- Integrating cross-functional collaboration
- Automating
- Unlocking data across the organization
- Reorganizing your resourcing structure

However, a number of things can work against you when it's time to re-platform, update, or launch a new product. You might have to deal with competition, settle internal squabbles, manage labor issues, load up on talent, or solve time constraints, to name a few. There may even be geo-political issues at play, and other forces that seem intent on taking you out at the knees.

For your digital product transformation to succeed, you must understand what your audience needs, and be able to deliver better solutions than anyone else. To do this, it's essential to think about technology differently, and shift your mindset and strategy with an eye toward the following:

- Greater accessibility
- Streamlined systems of delivery
- An improved user experience
- Working from proof points (why, how, what, and when)

If you want to have the best people, you have to be willing to empower, coach, and provide them with opportunities to elevate their performance. Product managers work exceptionally hard to create value across companies. Still, there can be a disconnect when senior leaders don't understand the complexities involved in solving a particular challenge.

If you cannot address opportunities, aren't sure of the technologies involved, or lack a full appreciation of what's needed, you may be the hurdle that prevents product teams from successfully completing their work. This fact can breed misalignment, and put you in an uphill scramble at the start, such as:

- Being under-resourced/under-funded for success
- Taking on too many initiatives simultaneously

- Using unreliable/outdated methodologies
- Forcing rework (which can create time and budget overruns)

To avoid such circumstances, your digital product transformation needs to be about more than wanting to create great features, or building a better widget *just because*. It must address the true needs of your audience, and focus on creating the greatest impact possible. That's the path that leads to serving customers, and modernizing companies.

Leaders must focus on three aspects that differentiate platforms from one-offs: experience, application, and data. Each layer has its own life cycle, impact on investment planning, and role as a catalyst and/or enabler within a digital product transformation.

When viewing the experience, application, and data layers of a platform as a group, you gain a greater understanding of what it takes to own and lead a digital product transformation. This may be particularly relevant if you embrace Product Led Growth (PLG). Coined by OpenView Venture Partners, PLG is a growth model that focuses on the user, and views the product as the primary driver of customer acquisition, conversion, and expansion.[13]

By making the experience, application, and data layers part of your thinking, you begin to gain a greater sense of digital fluency that spans levels of strategy and execution. Without this fluency, it's easy to fall prey to hype, hope, and industry buzz. That's not to say that you must be an expert in every aspect of digital product transformation. However, it does help to recognize what you don't know. When you do, you can fill in knowledge gaps with the right people and support.

EXPERIENCE

Possessing a clear, succinct definition of what people mean when they talk about experience is imperative. Forrester Research simplified the definition of customer experience down to a single core statement: "How customers perceive their interactions with your company."[14] In other words, to say you focus on user experience (UX) means you care about providing a useful, usable, and enjoyable experience to every customer, across all devices and touchpoints. This translates to fulfilling the expectations you've set, and the promises you've made.

The experience layer of a platform addresses what it takes to meet the expectations and needs of users in every moment of their journey. It unifies the work you've done to deliver the right content, the architecture that organizes the display of information, and the paths that users follow to navigate your product. The experience layer also factors in their user flow (interactions, interface, accessibility considerations, etc.). Some common user flows include the following:

- Discovery (organic and/or paid channels)
- Introduction
- Education
- Demo/trial
- Sign up
- Paywall
- First-time use
- Onboarding
- Second-time & recurring use
- Product & service
- Account management
- Self-service support
- Facilitated customer support
- Retention & loyalty

At a technical level, the experience layer entails everything the user sees—the display logic, plus endpoint/client-side application functionality. Ideally, the experience layer is adaptive to evolving browsers, devices, and UX paradigms.

Consider a rideshare platform, for instance. The experience layer would involve mobile apps that are driver and rider centric, plus account management and/or administrative web interfaces. The life cycle of this layer is usually one to three years long, and typically accelerates to match the demands of users, as well as changes in your industry.

APPLICATION

The application layer addresses your business rules and logic, and enables the delivery and intake of data based on any given flow along a user's journey. While users rarely see the application layer, it is the engine that powers the entire experience.

The application layer addresses requirements for performance, including things like scale (as more users adopt the platform), compatibility, integration with cross-functional systems, process and automation points, and product maintenance. The application layer includes a number of core considerations, including:

- Inputs
- Outputs
- Functional logic
- Personalization (predictive intelligence)

It's common to have business rules and logic embedded within an API-first architecture—a codebase that splits the application architecture between server and endpoint. The server points the data through the API, while the endpoint handles things from there.

Using the rideshare example again, the application layer would be the logic that handles user authentication, assigns riders to drivers, calculates travel costs and duration, and handles the data transfer to all endpoints. The life cycle of the application layer usually lasts three to five years.

DATA

The data layer contains the application's data, which typically resides in a database, or another data storage system. It's worth noting that, in recent years, there has been a sizeable shift in software architecture to micro-servers, and serverless solutions. These new solutions break apart larger, more traditional systems, and deliver results that align with business domains and key functions. In our rideshare example, this would entail all rider and driver data, ride history, and payment information. Simple enough, right? Not quite.

Data is one of the most valuable assets any organization possesses. Therefore, you have to make sure your data layer is working for you. When you shift your thinking to see products as platforms, you discover how a product can enable data as a service within an organization. This creates a two-way, input/output dynamic, where you gather and use data to benefit your organization. This change in perspective can unlock incredible opportunities, and allow information between functions to move up and down through your business, and across your value chain. It can impact nearly everything, including:

- Source(s)
- Aggregation
- Processing
- Normalization
- Analysis
- Segmentation and association to audience
- Management
- Scalability
- Security

The most adept enterprises take the approach of data-as-a-service—consolidating and organizing data into one source of truth, then making it available to serve new and existing digital initiatives. Doing so unlocks data from legacy systems to drive new applications and digital platforms, without disrupting existing backend systems. Here are a number of common data sources that can enable your platform:

- Asset/content management (CMS)
- Enterprise resource planning (ERP)
- Identity management
- Marketing automation
- Customer relationship management (CRM)
- Point of sale (POS)
- Finance
- Production management
- Fulfillment (inventory control, shipping, customer service)

The life cycle of the data layer is often five to seven years. As long as your data is relevant to your business, you'll need to maintain and support the data layer at all costs.

SERVANT LEADERSHIP

> "When you have a top role, with a lot of people on the org chart under you, you have to work for them—not the other way around—if you want to lead. You need to step back, understand the goals, and question your agenda and habits every day. That's how you answer the question, 'What does the organization need, and how can I adapt so we go in the right direction?'"
>
> – Tatyana Mamut, CPO Nextdoor

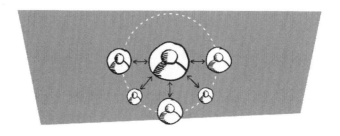

Successful leaders can draw from a library of tools, mechanisms, and experiences in order to adapt for the sake of the organization. They know that taking the opposite track—trying to force the organization to adapt to *their* needs—will not work. In fact, doing so is an ego-driven exercise that will eventually unravel. On the other hand, putting team members first is at the very root of what's known as servant leadership.

In theory, servant leadership sounds great. These days, it's something that a lot of people talk about. How often do leaders actually apply it? Where does it show up in organizations? Even in professional cultures where servant leadership is a reality, do employees know and embrace what it means for them? Would they agree that their leaders are working from a servant leadership mindset?

"A lot of people earn executive roles because they can be decisive," says Chris Cravens. "They make decisions quickly, often with very little information. However, if they get to the point where they don't take in new information, or aren't willing to change their opinion, that's a different thing."

In cases when empirical data opposes a leader's view, a leader—if they are working with a servant leadership mindset—will be able to take in new information, and modify their hypothesis or direction where necessary.

"That's a clear difference between having a strong, intentional point of view on something, and having an opinion that you want to follow simply because it's yours," says Cravens.

A servant leadership mindset puts leaders in a position to create cultures that inspire high-performance teams. We'll explore this in greater detail in Part Five. For now, it's important to note that inspiring others takes much more than just telling people that you work for them. In action, servant leadership gives workers the keys and confidence they need to lead the work. They know that you are there to apply a strategic lens when necessary, but they have the means to put their potential to full use, and work in alignment with your strategic foundation.

OPTIMISM VS. EXPECTATIONS

People appreciate knowing the truth, and leaders constantly find themselves walking the line between inspiring optimism, and keeping others grounded in realistic expectations. While optimism can be a powerful asset, what happens when an overly optimistic appraisal doesn't pan out? In many cases, optimism becomes disappointment.

The optimism vs. expectations paradox reminds me of a story I heard during a talk about navigating uncertainty. The speaker, the CEO of a multi-billion-dollar global company, was an extremely effective, positive person, known for infusing a high level of optimism into his leadership style. I expected he would talk about how optimism was the magic ingredient you need if you want to complete a large-scale transformation. Instead, he talked about what happens when people misinterpret optimism.

In his own experience, a group of influential shareholders misinterpreted his optimism as promises, and used it to set expectations. When things didn't pan out, his optimism actually prevented him from leading the company, and completing its transformation. Eventually, a core group of shareholders moved against him, and he was forced to step down. To this day, he's certain that things would have worked out differently if he'd been more cognizant of setting grounded expectations at the start.

Managing and balancing optimism and expectations is a challenge at any level, but especially for leaders. When you're leading others through a difficult or challenging experience, being as optimistic as possible may feel like the right thing to do. However, is that what others need? Or, do they need you to tether your optimism to concrete expectations? I believe the latter is true.

When you're overly optimistic, or stray from the path of your organization's strategic foundation, your optimism may actually create unrealistic expectations. If a product initiative goes south, people may point to your optimism and suggest that you set them up to fail. Even if that wasn't your intent, as soon as someone weaponizes optimism, it's no longer your story to tell.

Optimism is not antithetical to alignment. It can work in your favor, but may also work against you when it's out of touch with expectations.

TRUTH VS. REALITY

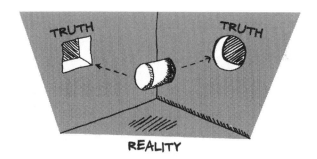

Unknowingly, many leaders create hurdles that compromise their ability to engage teams. This can happen when they push forward via a limited definition of truth, as opposed to considering a more well-rounded version of reality. Great leaders see the difference between truth and reality, and set aside cognitive and confirmation biases, in order to achieve deeper insight.

Confirmation bias happens when individuals create their own truth based exclusively on their perceptions, previous experiences, and the environment around them. These biases lead to inaccurate judgments, as well as illogical interpretations—broadly referred to as ungrounded thinking.

When leaders are stuck in confirmation bias, they seek out, interpret, and advocate for information that reinforces their existing beliefs. For an organization, this type of thinking runs counter to the goal of leveraging data and insight in order to inform smarter, more effective decisions. One of the most powerful ways to overcome confirmation bias is to rely on empathy. With empathy, you step into someone else's shoes, release biases, and seek to understand beyond the context of your limited view of the truth. When you lead with empathy, you demonstrate respect, and embrace the humanity of others—including employees, partners, customers, and users. Empathetic leaders ask:

- Who are you?
- What do you need?
- What do you see?
- What do you say and do?
- What do you hear, think, and feel about this situation?

Empathy is at the very heart of design thinking, and is a key component to building alignment. It allows you, as a leader, to cultivate contextual awareness that transforms the way you see a given situation, and extends your understanding beyond your earlier perceptions. With empathy, you build a better organization, and deliver impactful solutions that align with what people need.

THE NECESSITY OF BEING TRILINGUAL: BUSINESS + DESIGN + TECHNOLOGY

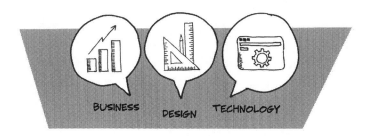

BUSINESS   DESIGN   TECHNOLOGY

Toward the end of Part Two, I introduced the importance of possessing a shared understanding that is rooted in a common language. Without a shared understanding, you run the risk of breeding misalignment. Your common language reinforces your shared understanding, and gives teams new ways to communicate, thereby increasing everyone's competence. As a result, your organization can move more efficiently as you build platform-minded solutions. Fostering a shared understanding is an essential part of your job as a leader. To do so, it helps if you can speak a few languages of your own, including those of business, design, and technology.

As I've stated before, it is important to know what you don't know. Believe it or not, many leaders overlook this fact, which can become a critical weakness. If you constantly ignore your deficiencies, or refuse to look for answers, you'll only make difficult situations worse. Your stubborn insistence on pushing forward, without a complete view of the terrain ahead, will cause you to invest in experiences and technologies that might *seem* good, but, in the end, will not create value for your organization, or satisfy users. You'll be leading with your ego, through the lens of your limited definition of the truth. In the process, you will wind up losing time, dumping money, and draining resources as you chase down a string of fragmented, high-risk, and overlapping digital product investments. Rather than setting the stage for a platform, you'll seek to complete initiatives in a patchwork manner—plugging holes instead of launching something that creates lasting value. Finally, the rate at which your organization deploys digital products in the future will slow down, and eventually grind to a stop.

Christie McAllister, the principal experience research manager of digital platform experience at Autodesk, is well aware of the extensive mental gymnastics involved in leading with alignment. "Sometimes, certain concepts that exist in one language or culture do not exist in another," she says. "The best thing a leader can do is to make a fairly close approximation."

In McAllister's years as a people-centered experience researcher and strategist, she's seen many projects where leaders possess a high fluency in one of the key languages—business, design, or technology—but not in the other two. "Some people, especially the more data-oriented, want things to be as concrete and specific as possible," she says. "My teams and I conduct bilateral, qualitative interviews. We try to understand what's important to the audience, what they already understand, and where they need support."

From there, McAllister and her teams begin filling out the narrative from a user's perspective. "We're always trying to understand the user," she says. To do so, she looks for connection points she can leverage in order to create a common language—terms, mental models, etc.—so multiple parties can understand one another, even when they have different areas of focus, diverse skillsets, and unique life experiences.

"In these cases, my job involves being a researcher, or a translator, who exists in both worlds," she says. "If that's what it takes to help us understand each other, then that's what we do."

Omri Gazitt, who has a 30-year track record of successful product and service delivery in the tech industry, approaches things from a similar perspective. He also delves into a deeper layer of how language propagates across internal levels of an organization.

"Often, through a process of accretion, organizations become their own bureaucracies," he says. "It's not much different than a product that goes through so many iterations that, after a while, it's impossible to trace the way back."

When Gazitt was at Microsoft, he was one of the first people to work on a new project that eventually became .NET. "I worked with brilliant people in the data access group," he says. "We were responsible for a ton of very mature data access technology. There was an entire ecosystem of tools and databases that were essentially connected through our technology."

Gazitt's team was charged with designing .NET's data access components. The team included 70 people, 30 of whom were developers. At one point, another development manager effectively called Gazitt onto the carpet, uncertain why Gazitt's team needed so many developers to maintain something that was essentially already done.

"At first, I was defensive," Gazitt recalls. "I was trying to protect my org. Why was this person asking me why we were so big, or wondering why we couldn't share resources? In the end, it was a completely legitimate question. I'd gotten so used to the way that the org defined itself—always having 70 people—I simply assumed that we *needed* 70 people to maintain things. I never contemplated another approach."

A situation like this often comes down to how you unpack, receive, explain, and reconsider information. A related challenge points back to size, scale, and sprawl, which Gazitt became familiar with at Microsoft.

"The type of thinking that supports resource allocation in leaner organizations doesn't always take root in larger ones," he says. "Those places usually measure success, power, or prestige by how many people you have. Even if you look at a company like Google, which is known for being spartan in how it allocates resources and people, you still see similar power struggles."

To Gazitt's point, turf wars happen in many organizations, particularly when managers become over-protective of resources. "You start measuring the size of your domain by the number of people involved," he says. In organizations where the primary cost is people—not processes, materials, or inventory—it can be difficult for leaders to care about being fluent in business, design, and technology. However, when they can speak these languages, they set themselves apart in the digital space, and are more prepared to lead with alignment.

"I remember talking to Satya Nadella, Microsoft's current CEO," Gazitt recalls. "Back when he was leading the business applications division, they acquired a company that had really wonderful people and technology. There was a debate over whether they should just use what was in .NET. The new team was reluctant. They had invented their own baby. Satya told the .NET team to find homes for these people. They were brilliant, and the .NET team would learn something from them. He knew that their input could help the .NET design frameworks. Of course, the .NET division was all too happy to do so."

In Gazitt's view, which is one I share, Nadella made a key decision that incorporated aspects of business, design, and technology. "He was thinking like an entrepreneur, a much broader way than people in other orgs were doing at the time," Gazitt says.

This type of thinking is possible when leaders can apply trilingual fluency to their decision-making process. It leads to keener insights, broader perspectives, and a deeper understanding of opportunities.

FOCUS ON THE RIGHT THINGS AT THE RIGHT TIME

Leaders face the daunting challenge of guiding teams through developing new products, services, and delivery models in a constantly evolving digital environment. Being trilingual in your thinking helps you know what to focus on, and when to focus on it, so you can develop clear, coherent steps forward. For instance, if you focus exclusively on data, but overlook key aspects of experience and application—whether knowingly or otherwise—you may create misalignment, and set your organization up for failure.

Maria Giudice is the founder and design leader of Hot Studio, and co-author of *Rise of the DEO*. She has run agencies, led global client-side teams, and supported startups for more than two decades. In her words, she has seen her share of clients, big and small, start with lofty dreams that never come true. At the core of these situations, she often finds leaders who lack trilingual fluency.

"The majority of these dreams do not make it," she says. "Or, if they come to life, they sputter out. I have worked with many startups over the course of my professional career, and only a handful have made it."

There are plenty of reasons, along with troves of research, data, case studies and testimonials, that explain why some companies and products make it, and others do not. In Giudice's experience, it often has to do with the person or people leading the initiative, and a series of common mistakes she sees happen.

"Some leaders look at the market, find an opportunity, identify an audience, focus on the pain point, and target the market size," she says. "Then they think, 'Something's here! Let's double down, launch our product, and see how it goes.'"

While there's nothing wrong with such exuberance at the start, when leaders overlook critical challenges as the process ramps up, issues will point back to how well they understood—or didn't understand—places where business, design, and technology intersect. In an effort to maintain optimism, they focus on the shiny object, but overlook what customers and users want. As they remain bullish on their idea, and tune out other voices, they create a fatal level of misalignment.

"On the surface, you might indeed have a great idea," Giudice says. "Perhaps you package it in a solid business model. The market may be ideal. However, timing might still be the magic bullet you're missing. I've seen plenty of great ideas arrive too early, particularly during the dot-com era. Users simply weren't ready."

Many mistakes happen in the early phases of defining a product, and validating how desirable, feasible, and viable it is. "Early mistakes often happen with prototypes," Giudice says. "Many things can go wrong. Some people don't do prototypes at all. They think they have to get their minimally viable product—MVP—out there. I love 'agile,' but there's a danger when people don't understand what agile means. They can wind up skipping steps because they try to get something to market as quickly as possible."

Launching a digital product just to get it *out there* is never the right move. Leaders must take ownership of the process, and not rush a product. Otherwise, teams will indeed skip steps, or overlook key insight and validation they would otherwise gain from experimentation and prototyping. Rushing ahead can put you on a course where you abandon your vision, or fall out of alignment with what otherwise may have been a successful endeavor. Without experimentation, plus a proof of concept and/or prototype, it becomes difficult to gauge how well any product aligns with the market. Among other things, you miss an opportunity to gather feedback, and discover how functional the product is within the context of the larger ecosystem of related products and services.

"When you throw down real money too fast, you put blinders on," Giudice says. "You might know that your idea isn't so great, but you've invested too much money to walk back to the beginning." In cases like these, organizations fall prey to trying to conform results to a faulty vision, rather than adapt the vision around what needs to happen. You wind up dumping more money and resources in the hopes that things turn around. When leaders become overly focused on deliverables, and forget about outcomes, this can be a warning sign of pending failure.

"Companies will say things like, 'Well, we have a plan to build it, so let's build it. We'll follow our plan regardless,'" says John Mullins, associate professor of management practice at London Business School. "You could be building a product, or launching a company. If it doesn't ultimately meet the needs of customers, then it won't go anywhere. The fundamental piece is to deliver something that customers actually want to buy."

"What leaders don't realize is that once they start engaging product managers, engineers, and designers, you don't just give birth and leave the baby at the fire station," says Giudice. "You are creating a digital organism that will constantly evolve. There's a lack of awareness of just how much money, effort, and people you need in order to get a product to the marketplace, and then sustain it."

Upon launch, promotion can become a major issue that some leaders overlook until it's too late. "Plenty of smart organizations don't fully understand PR and marketing, or how to acquire customers," Giudice says. "Does your product or business model have a strategy to acquire new customers, while cultivating the customers you currently have?" In many ways, issues such as these refer back to how well leaders can embrace change—and also change their own minds. The truth is, being overly rigid will obstruct the path of any digital product transformation. It can happen at any point, regardless of how big or small the change is. Leaders don't always need to take giant steps to make major changes. Still, even baby steps can induce a certain amount of fear, and require flexibility in thinking and actions.

To lead with alignment, and deliver products and services that make an impact, you must be willing to alter the way you approach planning, designing, developing, promoting, launching, and maintaining. You must also be accountable to the right things at the right time, and willing to ask questions such as the following:

- Why are we doing this?
- How will this improve things for customers?
- What are we missing, not seeing, or not listening to?
- Where in the workflow does a problem exist?
- What does my team need to move forward?
- Who within (or outside of) our organization is best equipped to address this situation?
- How do we prioritize the need to address this problem, in relation to other priorities?
- How will our work here affect the customer/user?
- Do we need to go backwards before we go forward, to make sure we're not missing something?

REVISIT YOUR RELATIONSHIP WITH DATA: TRANSACTIONAL VS. BEHAVIORAL

Our understanding of data is fundamental to business transformation, digital product performance, and continued improvement. I'd like to explore the relationship between two types of data: transactional and behavioral. Leaders need to understand the difference between them if they're going to lead with alignment.

Businesses and organizations have been gathering transactional data for decades. It provides important logistical information related to what people buy, how they purchase it, when it ships, etc. This information sheds light on purchasing habits, but doesn't tell us why people buy what they buy, or how they use it. That's one reason why mining mounds of transactional data is not enough. Leaders must recognize and understand how and why people choose and use certain products and services. This insight comes from behavioral data.

Consider the case of milkshakes for breakfast. If you're familiar with Clayton Christensen's Jobs to be Done theory and framework, then you may already know the story.[15] A major fast-food chain wanted to improve milkshake sales. They focused their marketing efforts on the product—hyping its thickness, for instance—and demographics, via the help of customer surveys. However, sales did not improve.

When Christensen and his research team came in, they discovered that 40% of all milkshake sales happened in the morning, and that customers tended to order them in the drive-thru lane. This next level of transactional data gave them something to dive into in search of the *why*. However, the company was satisfied with the data, and jumped back into chasing their next round of assumptive hunches. As they saw it, all they had to do was bang the drum about how great their milkshakes were. This time, they simply correlated these high points to enjoying a milkshake in the morning. Their efforts failed again.

As Christensen went back to work on the data, he uncovered something that the marketers had not considered—the job of the morning milkshake was to satisfy consumers who needed to feel sated and satisfied until lunch. They were buying milkshakes because they had not eaten breakfast, were in mid-commute, and needed to power through their first few hours of work.

Once the company revisited the way they understood the need, they began to get a clearer view of the actual competition. It wasn't ice cream sandwiches, or other drive-thru milkshakes. It was breakfast bars, protein shakes, and on-the-go yogurt. This behavioral understanding helped them shift their messaging away from 'we have the creamiest milk-shake,' to 'we have the best, most convenient morning meal for your commute.' Understanding this correlation helped create strong results for the client, and also opened the doors to new discoveries.

Delving into behavioral data is key if you want to lead with alignment. It helps answer *how* and *why* people choose a product or service, and provides you with new ways to move beyond assumptions, empathize with customers, and connect with their true needs. That's not to say that transactional data isn't useful, because it is. However, transactional data alone should not drive new promotions, or spearhead a change initiative. If you don't find out *why* sales spike, or *how* users engage with your product, you'll never decode the full story.

When you think about a product and the people involved in its existence and evolution, you must understand the product's purpose, and the job that users want the product to perform. If business leaders are compelled to solve problems simply by throwing new technology at them, they are only scratching the surface of the job they need the technology to do. They see a problem and a solution, but not the gulf of uncertainty and unanswered questions between the two.

Leaders who make the final purchasing decision may not understand the complexity of the job, or the technology at all. They may overlook potential errors on the user input side, or possess an incomplete picture of what product managers and teams need in order to deliver. Without seeking a deeper understanding, it's impossible to create a strong, platform-minded product strategy.

The reason why so many digital product transformations fail doesn't always point back to being underfunded, or spread too thin. Plenty of organizations continue to stick with broken or antiquated thinking and methodologies, often because they don't know another way. Again, delving into behavioral data can be the key that gets you out of an old box. The insight you glean allows you to pursue a more well-rounded reality of what's going on for customers/users.

Imagine that your company is updating a critical tool that supports the way you serve customers. Here are a few questions to ask and answer before you start:

- What job must the new solution perform?
- Why is the current solution not fulfilling its job?
- How do we know our assessment is valid? Have we evaluated the right things, and in the right way?
- Why is this new solution the answer?
- How will the new solution change the way that teams interact with customers?
- How will we measure success during the transition from the old to the new?
- How will we measure success once the new solution is launched?
- Have we aligned our expectations correctly?
- Is the product/tool aligned with our organizational mission and vision?

"Answering questions like these is where much of the work occurs," says Jared Spool. "When you get into complex problems, things become harder to research. It takes a lot of effort and investment. It's not a matter of waving your hand and finding an answer."

In the end, if your goal is to build a cost-effective solution that aligns with what users need, you must be willing to explore new models that will impact the way your organization executes.

PLANNING IS NOT STRATEGY

"A good and simple definition of a strategy is that it's a way to get from where you are today, to where you want to go. First, you have to pick out where you're trying to go. What's your north star? What will success look like? Then, you pick your time period. Is it five years? Something else? To win the game, you have to start by defining the game you're playing."

– Jim Gochee, former CPO, New Relic

In Part Two, I mentioned that many leaders confuse planning with strategy, or think they are the same things. This costly misconception is one that leaders cannot afford. Returning to the relationship between the two, let's explore how they impact your ability to lead with alignment.

PLANNING THROUGH A LEADERSHIP LENS

For leaders, plans are made up of tactics that define exactly what you're going to do, when you're going to execute on them, and what follows next. Essentially, your plan says 'if we follow XYZ, we'll attain success—as long as we keep moving forward.' This definition sounds a lot like Jim Gochee's quote about strategy above. However, to reiterate some of what I shared in Part Two, plans rarely account for unknowns, changes, or new priorities. They say 'go forward,' but they don't tell you how to start, what to look for, or how to shift gears when the landscape changes. Nor do plans provide a framework for critical decision making. A plan without a strategic foundation gives people a false sense of clarity and security, which can lead to misalignment, and create failure.

In his book, *Inspired*, Marty Cagan talks about the root causes of failed product efforts through the lens of how organizations approach the work of building product strategies. "I see the same basic way of working at the vast majority of companies, of every size, in every corner of the globe," Cagan writes.[16] What he's noticed is that most companies are prepared to march forward with their plans, but only *successful* companies build strategies around unique insights.

STRATEGY THROUGH A LEADERSHIP LENS

For leaders, a strategy provides a succinct and tangible definition of where you're going, the challenges to overcome, the approach you'll take to get there, and the value you'll create. It tells you *where* to focus, and explains *why* it matters. Your strategy also empowers teams, and triggers higher-level performance across the organization. With a strategy, people and workgroups focus on the right things, and are prepared to shift into delivering a great product or service.

One misconception I've discovered is that many organizations believe that the only thing they need in order to push through an initiative is a great culture. Culture may be invaluable, but if the organization is moving in the wrong direction, is misaligned, or lacks a sound strategy, then it is never enough. In fact, pinning your hopes on culture alone will hinder your business transformation, and derail digital product efforts. However, one way to maximize your culture is to align it with your strategy.

"I've done a lot of research on strategy," says Jim Gochee. "We had, I would say, an informal strategy for the first seven years at New Relic. Then, we created a formal strategy that we published internally. Writing and publishing it brought more people on board."

By formalizing a strategy, leaders help teams understand and track the steps they must take in order to move forward. They can also revisit these steps periodically, at any point during the process. "We had an early self-service strategy at New Relic," Gochee recalls. "Mostly, it involved how we serviced smaller companies. About a year before we went public, we changed our strategy. We were getting so much interest from enterprise companies, we decided to pivot in their direction."

To do so, Gochee's team had to pause, develop a new strategy, and identify the approach that would help them transition into being the best standard tool of choice for enterprise customers. They had to revisit marketing, selling, product design, and development, because they knew that enterprise customers had significantly different needs and expectations than small businesses. What New Relic discovered was that, as they started to pivot, they still hadn't articulated their strategy.

"Some teams were already pushing to enterprise clients," Gochee recalls. "Others kept doing what they'd been doing for smaller customers. We weren't aligned on an end-vision. Plus, teams hadn't seen a strategy that involved them and their work."

Despite New Relic's strong culture, their fragmented strategy created misalignment. The same can happen in any organization, regardless of culture, when trying to pivot without having an aligned strategy in place. It's similar to when a product has a strong, early market fit. Things might feel right at first, but there's more work to do. Eventually, all organizations must identify and fill gaps in order to keep moving. From Gochee's perspective, customers often hold the answers.

"I don't think product teams spend enough time with customers," he says. "They're not getting feedback regularly. When they do, they're getting it too late in the process, and can't act on customer insight." You see this often with startups, or organizations where passionate leaders drive decisions. Their energy and enthusiasm might catalyze momentum, but these personalities must be tempered with the willingness to seek and listen to feedback, even if and when the message says they're on the wrong track.

Plenty of product managers possess a similar mentality when it comes to a digital product transformation. That's another reason why leaders at all levels need to check egos at the door. In a best-case scenario, all team members will get excited about the work, but will also stay open to the possibility that something may be misaligned.

"Pushback can come from any direction," Gochee says. "I've seen it at the product manager level, with engineers, sales, etc. Sometimes, it comes when your customer support team is adamant about something they keep hearing during calls. Leaders can thrive when they build a culture that sets a vision, but also stays open to the fact that they may need to update the vision at key moments."

ALIGNING STRATEGY & EXECUTION

Your strategic foundation is imperative to achieving alignment. Part Four will expand the strategy discussion, and focus primarily on building a strategic foundation. As we wrap up Part Three, it's worth taking a look at strategic foundations through the lens of leading with alignment.

A strategic foundation is how a leader provides clarity, builds team focus, informs better decisions, accelerates the speed of delivery, and spurs collaboration. Even if you have the world's greatest idea, you need a strategic foundation if you want teams to execute and deliver.

Your strategic foundation is key when it's time to shift from strategy to defining the right solution, and moving forward with effective execution, which is not an easy process. It requires alignment, excellent communication, and a culture that supports change. This is where having a winning strategy will help you develop and follow a plan that focuses on deploying appropriate capabilities, processes, tools, and resources at the right time.

Leaders, managers, and team members all have many decisions to make across the product development life cycle. With your strategic foundation in place, everyone will have an easier time forging a path that leads to success. As teams work to prioritize issues, and develop solutions, your strategic foundation provides key information that ensures you are working on the right things. Your foundation guides your thinking when it's time to build teams and set benchmarks related to creating, executing, and supporting your product. This understanding will help you define a clearer picture when assigning key roles and responsibilities, exploring solutions, mapping out interdependencies, and strengthening links between people, processes, and systems that will bring your product to market.

You will also put yourself in a better position relative to timing. For instance, when an organization develops a business case prematurely, or does so without enough insight, the project often falls apart. However, when executed at the right time, and with the right information, a business case will define and outline the true potential, and draw a realistic picture of the investment ahead. This information brings complexities to the forefront, so you can get ahead of them.

As you continue to define your digital product transformation, you can also document requirements, and address key business, design, and technical considerations essential to delivery. Your strategic foundation will become a powerful advantage that provides critical insight, galvanizes your efforts, and empowers people to be their best in any role. Even as the market decides the next generation of winners and losers, your foundation helps you take control of your success.

PART FOUR
ALIGNMENT & STRATEGIC FOUNDATIONS

The need for clarity

- Build your common language and shared understanding
- Emphasize team focus and decision making
- Collaborate, accelerate, and evaluate

Building a strategic foundation

Strategic foundation messaging framework

Five elements of the strategic foundation

- Vision
- Challenges
- Outcomes
- Actions
- Measures

Strategic foundation across the product development life cycle

PART FOUR

Alignment & Strategic Foundations

"We are stubborn on vision. We are flexible on details."

— Jeff Bezos, founder and CEO, Amazon

Attempting to define or demystify strategy has become its own sub-genre in the world of professional articles and business books. Many authors tell us what strategy *isn't*. For instance, we know that strategy is not any of the following, though a strong strategy will align with, reflect, and even guide these foundational aspects:

- Ambition
- Mission
- Vision
- Core values
- Objectives
- Goals
- Forecasting
- Planning
- Solutions

Other authors focus on the distinction between *good* and *bad* strategy. In the words of Richard Rumelt, "bad strategy has a life and logic of its own."[17] If Rumelt's assertion is accurate, then right now, there's a business leader out there successfully building a bad strategy that a team is about to follow. One reason that bad strategy happens is because leaders see strategy through the lens of setting performance goals. However, strategy must align with things like solving problems, and responding to challenges. Rumelt writes that good strategy "is a way through a difficulty, an approach to overcoming an obstacle, a response to a challenge. If the challenge is not defined, it is difficult or impossible to assess the quality of the strategy."[18]

Plenty of digital product initiatives begin with a vision of the future, and a set of ambitious goals. However, they overlook actual user-related problems, or market challenges. I know of many cases where leaders and managers start a product initiative by telling teams to execute on a loosely defined idea, or a list of deliverables in order to create a new feature set. This type of poor strategic direction is based on goals, but does not address *why* or *how* the product initiative matters. Such an approach rarely, if ever, creates alignment. Forcing talented people to follow a list of requirements just to build something is a shortsighted trap that will undermine effective strategy, and dramatically increase the risk of failure.

I'm reminded of a story about Bill Campbell, a major force in building many Silicon Valley giants, including Apple, Google, and Intuit. He was at Intuit when they were moving into banking products. In one situation, a product manager presented the engineers with a list of features that a new product *needed* to possess. Campbell threatened to toss the manager out on the street.[19] His reaction wasn't about his ego, or the need to throw his weight around. He was setting a very specific check and balance. The engineers needed to focus on solving actual problems—product features would come *after* they understood the needs of consumers and users, not *before*.

THE NEED FOR CLARITY

Clarity is imperative if you want to build a strong, effective strategy. To possess clarity in the digital space, you have to begin by defining your current state, then mapping out a path that leads to your desired destination. What are you trying to solve? Why are you trying to solve it? Once solved, what will your future state look like? This type of thinking spurs alignment, and helps you establish a foundation for good strategy and team performance.

Without clarity, you'll never build alignment at every level, or move from strategy, to solution, to execution. Instead, your people may be stuck pecking away at lists of deliverables—focused on features and performance goals without knowing why they matter. Product teams should never be stuck just building features—they need to be solving problems. To do so, they must first understand the problems, and apply their insights into creating the strategies that solve them.

Strategic clarity drives team focus, informs decisions, accelerates the speed of delivery, and inspires effective collaboration. It is a must if you are going to answer key questions, including the following:

- Why are things the way they are?
  o How do we define our current state?
  o What events or decisions have led to this current state?

- What problems must we solve to move forward?
  - What are the symptoms?
  - What are the root causes?
- What other challenges exist because of this problem?
  - How do these challenges affect customers/users?
  - How do these challenges impact our people, processes, and resources?
- What must change in order to solve the challenge?
  - What can we do now to get started?
  - Once completed, what will our future state look like?

The importance of clarity cannot be overstated when it comes to building a strategic foundation. Its existence—or absence—will be felt in every aspect of how teams operate. If you can't explain the strategy in a simple way, then it's possible that you don't fully understand the problem, and/or how to solve it. Without clarity, your initiative will suffer from misalignment, and head toward failure. Let's look at three ways you can infuse clarity into your strategic foundation.

1. BUILD YOUR COMMON LANGUAGE AND SHARED UNDERSTANDING

The connection between clarity and a common language is a two-way street. On one end, the drive for clarity prompts teams to generate and work from a system that includes a shared common language, be it phrases, codes, or a mutual understanding of what certain words and steps mean. On the other end, the common language, once created, reinforces clarity, and accelerates performance.

Product managers and leaders must help build, strengthen, and demonstrate the importance of a common language. In addition, they must ensure that teams possess and use a common language that corresponds with their organization's greater language set. Otherwise, it's possible that workgroups or individuals will interpret key terminology differently from one another. It will be like playing the telephone game at an organizational level. As phrases move from mouth to mouth, their meanings will change. Five interpretations later, no one will know what anything means.

Below, I've included a few terms that get tossed around to the point where they can lose their meaning altogether. They become buzzwords, just as easy to say as they are to dismiss. If you're using them, be sure that the people in your organization share an understanding of what they mean:

- Accessibility
- Agile
- Brand
- Data
- Engagement
- Innovation
- Customer experience
- Prototype
- Roadmap

While possessing a shared language is a cultural concern for many organizations, actively building one is a discipline you must include as part of organizational design. "To be able to connect the big and the small, people need the same information," says John Mullins. "The same goes for trying to empower marketers, managers, researchers, designers, and engineers to be passionate about understanding the meaning behind their work."

To achieve this, Mullins refers to strategy as a framework that demonstrates a shared understanding, including a common language. "Without a framework, I might look at something that you provide, and interpret it in a way that's entirely different from how you interpret it," he says. "However, when there's a shared understanding, we can interpret things the same way."

Your common language can work like a baseline that gives people and groups a starting place from where they can explore interpretations. As you seek clarity, your common language can include a verification mechanism, allowing people to validate the fact that they are on the same page. This can be as simple as asking questions at the end of a hallway sidebar, so people can reflect and verify that they understand one another.

2. EMPHASIZE TEAM FOCUS AND DECISION MAKING

It's difficult to build and maintain confidence throughout every phase of a digital product transformation. How do you know you're making the right decisions? Do you trust the information that's available? What if the information is limited? To manage moments of uncertainty and doubt, clarity helps teams stay focused at key times, which can galvanize their confidence.

As teams identify solutions and work toward outcomes, your strategic clarity helps everyone keep priorities straight along the way. With this level of clarity, team members and stakeholders can focus on what they need—and when they need it—as they create, execute, iterate, and support one another at every step. As they explore solutions together, you will start to recognize opportunities where people, processes, and systems align in new ways.

When it comes to making decisions with confidence, clarity—combined with your strong strategic foundation—creates a powerful advantage. Team members can leverage critical insights, get more out of their efforts, and empower one another to be their best. As you move closer to your desired outcome, clarity will continue to inspire confidence, whether people are documenting requirements, or addressing key business, design, and technical considerations.

3. COLLABORATE, ACCELERATE, AND EVALUATE

Are the right people involved when they need to be? Are new skills and talents rising to the surface? In order to achieve greater collaboration, everyone must be clear about what they're doing, why they're doing it, and what certain outcomes should look like. Possessing clarity will improve collaboration, build alignment and trust, establish accountability, and provide an understanding of what it takes to move forward. When everyone agrees to the rules of the game, it aligns expectations, and propels initiatives.

Many product teams become entrenched in a cycle where leaders measure performance based exclusively on the speed of delivery. They may have giant feature sets they want to create, but lack clarity regarding what customers want. These teams will eventually get bogged down with product backlogs, or miss other opportunities.

With clarity, collaborative teams can move away from worrying about how fast they produce features, and focus on key variables—such as research, design thinking, and value creation—that help drive outcomes. When leaders reinforce the fact that listening and learning matter, teams feel free to ask questions, seek insight, and address unknowns. Working from this mindset will boost collaboration, and actually accelerate the speed of delivery.

The clarity that comes from building your strategic foundation also helps you establish a set of criteria with which you can evaluate decisions as you go forward with product development. This criteria prepares you to ask key questions that will help you identify the right solution to the problem you're addressing, including the following:

- Does it align with the organization's mission, purpose, brand, and values?
- Will it solve the problem we want to address?
- Is the solution desirable, feasible, and viable, based on known constraints?
- Will it enable us to deliver the intended outcome for customers and/or users?
- Will it enable us to deliver the intended outcome for the organization?
- Can we measure and report on progress?

Being able to answer these questions in the affirmative is a sign that you are working from alignment. If you cannot answer 'yes,' then you either need to dig deeper to address why not, or rule out your solution and move on. Doing so will help to ensure that you're working on the right things at the right time.

BUILDING A STRATEGIC FOUNDATION

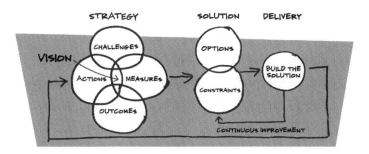

Creating and launching digital products or services, then successfully versioning them once they're in the world, are significant undertakings. To accomplish this, you must have a strategic foundation. Unfortunately, many managers and executives lack the deep-rooted expertise they need to select new technologies, lead integration initiatives, and understand potential domino effects at every stage. These leaders can overlook the fact that the true costs of transformation and integration go beyond the bottom line, and include the hours spent orchestrating, managing, iterating, configuring, and supporting the new product. Yet, they move forward anyway, either with a bad strategy, or no strategy at all.

There are many types of strategies—pricing, go-to-market, retention, etc. I'd like to focus on some of the foundational aspects that successful strategies possess. For instance, you want to identify the right opportunity, select where and when to compete, and solve problems for customers in unique, sustainable ways. However, as I've stated elsewhere, confusion exists when it comes to how strategy differs from planning. One succinct way to highlight the difference is that **plans** include tactics that say what you'll do, when you'll execute, and what follows next, while **strat-**

egy defines where you're going, the approach you'll take, and the value you'll create in a tangible way.

Recall back to the four levels of alignment I introduced in Part One: Individual, Team, Organizational, and Market. Your strategic foundation facilitates alignment between all four. Most importantly, it clarifies the following five elements, which we'll explore in greater detail starting in the next section:

- Vision
- Challenges
- Outcomes
- Actions
- Measures

Strategy starts the moment you begin to explore an idea. Perhaps your goal is to provide a platform that improves the way people work, or unlocks the speed at which they collaborate. Imagine trying to create a strategic foundation, or get stakeholder buy-in, without having clarity, vision, or direction. The early stages of building a strategic foundation may read something like this:

- You identify a challenge or unique opportunity, and >
- You have an idea about how to address it. To explore it, you >
- Survey the marketplace. This involves >
- Uncovering potential needs and barriers (buyers, users, supply chain, competitors, regulations, etc.). You begin to >
- Hone your idea into something that feels more tangible. To get to the next step, you >
- Form a hypothesis of how your idea will address the challenge or unique opportunity, and >

- Begin the work involved in validating the idea (product). During this phase you >
- Identify the end-state, which helps you gain new levels of clarity. You also >
- Decide whether or not there's an equitable value exchange going forward. If there is value in going forward, then you >
- Define that value exchange, which helps you >
- Anchor to what you need (internally and externally) in order to achieve it, and scale over time. However, if the answer to the question of an equitable value exchange is 'no,' you >
- Pivot, >
- Begin focusing on different problems, or >
- Start over.

Visually, it may play out as follows:

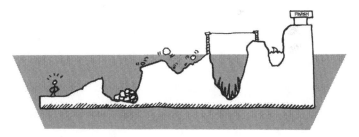

While a strategy may come out of this process, it doesn't mean that you're done. As you set the stage for deploying the right capabilities, processes, tools, and resources, you'll distill down to a more precise version of your strategic foundation. It may read something like this example of a strategic foundation framework:

STRATEGIC FOUNDATION MESSAGING FRAMEWORK

FOR

Company

TO ACHIEVE

Vision Statement (the destination that moves forward
the company's mission)

WE NEED TO SOLVE

Challenges (the current state)

BY FOCUSING ON

Priority (your approach)

WE CAN PRODUCE

Intended near-term customer outcome

AND

Intended near-term business outcome (future state)

WE CAN DO THIS BY

Taking these immediate and coherent actions

AND MEASURING OUR

Forward progress indicators

This simple framework is merely a model for distilling your strategic foundation into a single statement. The deeper, substantive work goes on in the background, and helps you arrive at this type of message. When you truly understand your strategy, this framework will help you communicate it effectively. By doing this work, leaders assume responsibility for developing the clarity, focus, and rules of the game that product teams need to know if they're going to solve problems, create momentum, and produce successful results.

With your strategic foundation in place, you and your teams will be able to forge an adaptive, grounded plan that establishes a path forward, and helps you focus on the right opportunities that move you ahead—from inception through delivery.

A great strategic foundation is a living thing. Its role goes beyond bringing the product to market (though this might be an expected outcome or goal). Your strategic foundation speaks to the product's value in the world. This includes explaining how it aligns with your business strategy, and how it will serve your user. Keep in mind that strategy is episodic. You will need to revisit it after each major milestone throughout the development life cycle. It will evolve many times before it becomes a discipline that others adhere to, practice, and reference in the future.

FIVE ELEMENTS OF THE STRATEGIC FOUNDATION

Let's return to the five elements I mentioned above, which make up your strategic foundation: Vision, Challenges, Outcomes, Actions, and Measures. Combined, they empower people and teams to work in alignment.

VISION: This is the clearly defined and measurable long-term goal you wish to achieve, and your intended destination. Your vision acts as your true north. You may not have all the answers on how you will get there just yet, but your vision is your focus. Everyone's efforts go into realizing the vision, and every iteration of your product brings you one step closer. In some cases, your product vision might be the same as your company vision; in others, it might be specific to a business unit, or a suite of products and services that enables the company to achieve new goals and fulfill its mission (purpose).

Your vision needs to be inspirational, specific, and measurable. More than anything, you want your vision to answer two key questions:

1. Do you know, and can you articulate, the overarching goal you wish to achieve?
2. Does the vision align with your company's purpose, core values, and direction?

Your answers will reinforce the drive behind your product initiative, whether you wish to solve something internally, or create a solution for the market. As your product evolves with each iteration, you'll want to revisit your vision, explore it through new lenses, and apply a business discipline that involves testing how well it aligns with your organizational direction. Doing so will help you determine whether it's time to push forward, or pivot.

"If you can't anchor your product's strategic foundation to the *why* of your company—your mission—then you're already missing the big picture," says Katherine Nester, chief product and technology officer at Ruby Receptionists. "Everything you're doing must be anchored to the bigger purpose. This will help everyone involved, across every function of the company. It turns *we* and *I* into a very powerful *us*."

Understanding and connecting the *why* of your product to that of your business is a critical first step in alignment. Not doing so will lead to misalignment, and turn your initiative into a poor investment. It may even point to underlying issues at the organizational level.

"Part of your job as a product leader is to keep people aligned with the problem you're trying to solve," Nester says. "However, if you're also trying to solve tomorrow's problem, and the next problem, and the next problem after that, you'll end up building things you don't need."

Navigating this terrain within your strategic foundation, and anchoring it to your organizational purpose, will help stakeholders and teams stay aligned. To do so, it's important to explore what makes a product's strategic foundation successful.

Even when leaders value their organization's purpose, many underestimate how important it is for the product's strategy to align with the larger vision. Some abandon the process of aligning purpose, strategy, and vision too soon. Others simply skip doing this essential work. And, far too many arrive at a 'good enough' strategic foundation that doesn't connect critical pieces. A great product strategy needs a clearly defined vision in order to:

- Communicate a shared organizational vision and mutual understanding that people and teams can rally around.
- Address assumptions head on, and navigate the unknown.
- Prompt and answer important questions.
- Enable people to make smart decisions.
- Demonstrate the link between ideas, strategies, solutions, and approaches as you work toward delivery.

In many cases, leaders think of vision statements in terms of whether or not they are inspirational enough. That's not the whole story of a vision statement—especially not product vision statements. A successful vision will clearly communicate future objectives, thereby informing and guiding decisions related to branding, product development, recruitment, resource allocation, organizational planning and more.

As you build a strategic foundation for your product or service, you must align it with the bigger picture. Here is a simple example of anchoring your product and company visions:

In order to fulfill our **organizational mission** of eliminating child hunger, and scale to supporting three million families over the next seven years, **we must enhance**

our digital portal in order to **improve the speed and efficiency** with which we support community members who seek access to education and food sources.

As this example illustrates, your focus must be on communicating a shared understanding of how the new product will enable long-term goals so the organization can fulfill its mission. Your product vision must communicate, clearly and concisely, why the product or solution is needed, where you must focus, what's at stake, what you want to accomplish, and what long-term success looks like.

CHALLENGES: Your strategic foundation must clearly address the challenge(s) your product will solve. Doing so opens the door to your audience, uncovers how they are impacted by challenges, and differentiates between symptoms and root causes. In short, you must understand the current state, and the key moments that make up the sum of your audience's experience. As you define and diagnose challenges, you unlock key information that helps you understand the conditions that led to these challenges. This understanding roots your strategic foundation, and bolsters your product's market fit and advantage.

When you dedicate time to diagnosing the situation, it allows new types of thinking and inquiry to enter into your process. This, in effect, leads to completely different possibilities. You begin to see and understand things through new lenses, and gain insight into greater context. You also go beyond the surface of challenges, and understand the variables that will guide you toward defining actions, and arriving at solutions. In the process, your strategy evolves from good to great.

Connecting with your audience is one of the first steps to understanding the challenge and its impact, and thereby building alignment. When you call out core challenges, you possess greater context for the realities that these challenges present, and for the value in the solution you wish to create.

Let's consider the American inventor, Frederick McKinley Jones. In the late 1930s, Jones began exploring an idea that eventually led to cold chain innovations, and modern refrigeration.[20] However, when the idea first struck him, he wasn't planning to revolutionize the way that people stored, shipped, and delivered food across long distances. He'd been driving on a hot night, and started thinking about ways to cool the inside of his car. He was interested in comfort. Once he started iterating on his idea, he uncovered larger challenges that happened to involve transporting food and other perishable items.

By unlocking the idea's potential, and deepening its application, refrigeration and cold chain storage led to mass transformation across hundreds of markets, and thousands of products. Just think of the ways that refrigeration and cold storage impact the ability to transport medicine, blood, and donated organs, all of which are vital for the health and survival of millions of people every day. Jones could have stuck to creating comfort. Instead, he and others continued to push the idea, and uncover new challenges to solve.

Below are a few questions that can help you explore perceived problems or challenges in focused, aligned ways. Note their similarity to the questions I shared earlier, when discussing the need for clarity:

- What isn't working about the current situation?
- What does the future state look like if the situation doesn't change? How does it look if things do change?
- What are the costs of keeping things the same as they are now?
- What obstacles are in the way of realizing a better future state?

When you go deeper into any problem, you get clearer on what's possible. As you broaden your perspective, you help teams align and focus on new opportunities. Believe it or not, there are plenty of organizational leaders charging forward right now without understanding the scope of challenges involved. They're building business cases based on egos, biases, and assumptions, focused more on deliverables than outcomes. This mindset is one of the main reasons why organizations struggle when it's time to bring new digital experiences and technologies online, or complete major digital product transformations. They select a target without knowing whether or not it's right. They do not anchor into a well-defined strategy, nor do they diagnose challenges to the level required. Culturally, they may be determined to charge toward the finish, but they're either unwilling or unable to unpack the need, address the scope of the challenge, and confront the situation in a clear, definitive way.

In order to focus on challenges, you must understand the current state of affairs. Once you have this understanding of your audience, you can assess what business challenges you need to resolve to effectively identify and deliver the right solution. Consider some of the challenges that many businesses face right now:

- They lack an accurate picture of the customer journey.
- They need omnichannel customer engagement, education, and conversion.
- They cannot differentiate from competitors.
- They don't know how to personalize the customer experience, or improve performance across a buyer's journey.
- They are unable to expand into e-commerce and other digital offerings.
- They're struggling to implement self-service models that will reduce pressure on internal resources, and empower customers and partners.
- They must enable workflows across the organization, but don't know how to get started.
- They want to increase automation, real-time business intelligence, and the ability to scale sustainably, but are hesitant to disrupt the status quo.
- They need their people to have better access to actionable data.

Good strategy does not happen in a vacuum. It requires that you engage with audiences in order to understand their challenges, and explore internal challenges your business must address. When you do, you begin to see new points of view, which helps ensure the value you want to create.

One way to understand the challenges that customers face is to spend time connecting with them. Jim Gochee encourages his teams to check in with customers/users before they wrap up sales or service calls. His team members use informal conversations to find out how well the product is serving customers, whether or not their needs have changed, and even discover workarounds that customers/users are using. His teams use this information to clarify and validate the foundation of what they're building.

While conversations with customers/users may not be an option at every organization, having access to audiences can be extremely beneficial. That's why many successful product teams are becoming more outward-facing. Gathering feedback from customers and users can foster continuous discovery, shed light on new ideas, and steer all teams, including marketing, sales, and customer service, toward new opportunities.

With insight from your audiences, you can understand and uncover challenges in ways that help you identify one or more of the eight root causes of failure I listed in Part Two. From there, you can break down larger challenges into manageable, actionable issues, and dig deeper into their complexities. Here's an example of how a list of challenges may read:

> To **enhance our customer experience, increase personalization**, and **improve response times,** we must evolve from a static set of independent tools, to an integrated sales enablement and service delivery platform that empowers every employee. Challenges we have uncovered include:
>
> • Fragmented omnichannel customer experience
> • No contextual relevance
> • Missed opportunities for customer engagement

- Unrecognized upsell and cross-sell opportunities
- Too many distributed tools (offline/online)
- Duplicate work across tools with shared data
- Lack of a central data repository
- Inability to share common components
- No product and service personalization
- Limited automation of time-intensive tasks and processes
- Lack of version control
- No integration with other products
- Limited analysis capabilities and reporting
- Limitations of dynamically generated assets
- No feedback triggers
- No notifications to drive action or services
- No cumulative business intelligence

When your list of challenges is this comprehensive, you see things through an extremely broad lens, and recognize the interdependencies between each challenge. This sets the stage for what it will take to achieve intended outcomes, and the context for your approach. It may also unlock a wider application for your solution.

OUTCOMES: What is the future state, or near-term objective, your product must achieve? If successful, how will the product or platform help overcome known challenges, and deliver value to your audience? How well does your intended outcome track with your vision?

Generally speaking, there are two different outcomes to consider as your build your strategic foundation:

1. The intended outcome for customers/users who rely on your product or service. What value must you deliver in order to inform their behaviors?
2. The intended business outcome related to how the product will propel your organization forward. By serving customers and users, will the product also deliver a clear and compelling value that aligns with what your organization needs?

While your product vision articulates the big picture, outcomes focus on near-term (6-18 months) results that address the prioritized challenges and obstacles you must overcome. Identifying outcomes allows you to highlight short- and long-term benefits as the product evolves and scales. While your vision may be inspirational, your outcomes must be realistic and feasible. This is not to say that you cannot, or should not be aggressive; however, being inspiring is not a strategy, and effective performance requires clarity.

Your outcomes are *not* about accomplishing an arbitrary deadline, or satisfying someone's wish to create features. You must align your outcomes with priorities and resources that address your challenges. If not, you run the risk of building a poor and ineffective strategy. "It would be like not having strategic priorities at all," says Chris Cravens. "You'd just be leaving your teams confused."

You can generate outcomes in a step-by-step manner, asking questions at key increments. For instance:

- If we make decision X, and maintain priority Y, will it move us forward?
- Will this align us with the outcome we want for the user, and for the organization?

This process is not akin to solving a math equation. You may not arrive at an absolute answer every time—nor should you expect to. Instead, a strategically aligned foundation connects the dots, simplifies a complex ecosystem, creates focus, and promotes viability. This way, people and teams can safely explore ways to arrive at outcomes by solving known challenges, and uncovering new ones along the way.

For instance, you may have a chance to differentiate your product, increase user adoption, deepen retention, or expand into adjacent markets. Or, you may find that your organization is suddenly competing with a steep growth curve. The point is, objectives will change over time. Distilling them at key moments, and expanding them at others, is a natural process. Ensuring that they stay aligned with your strategy will help teams execute with precision.

"If you're constantly trying to manage the same list of data points on a regular basis, you're going to grind to a halt," Cravens says. "Instead, you can ask, 'What are the key outcomes and metrics we need to look at right now? How do we look at them quickly? How do we map this?'" Here is an example of a user outcome, followed by a product outcome:

User Outcome: Our unified platform will enhance the user experience via a simplified UX, increase community networking opportunities, and drive new levels of engagement, especially with self-service customers.

Product Outcome: With a unified platform, we will be able to build collective business intelligence, and add new benchmarking capabilities. This will enhance both upsell and cross-sell opportunities, and improve the way we market to existing customers. We can then extend the platform's services into key touchpoints, thereby enhancing the customer experience, and driving growth and retention.

Note that both statements refer back to customers/users. This points to the fact that even as you address multiple challenges, your outcomes will align.

ACTIONS: Your actions mark the broader approach, and the specific steps you will take as you move forward. They represent what needs to happen, and the interdependencies related to overcoming obstacles, and delivering the product. Actions reflect your vision, address challenges, and lead toward outcomes as you move from the current to the future state.

To paraphrase Richard Rumelt, even the smallest bit of strategy contains action. While a good strategy may not point out all of the actions at the start, it will provide clarity to help you identify what actions you must take along the way. In fact, the actions you wind up taking may not even be there at the beginning. Instead, they will come later, as you dig deeper into the need, understand the challenges, and identify an approach that will lead to your desired destination. Then, you will create a situation where actions align with, and reflect the work you've done, as well as the work you need to do.

Ideas don't always align with how well leaders understand the need, or the actions they encourage teams to take. That can happen when leaders skip the listening part, or focus exclusively on one aspect of a challenge. They may fall in love with ideas, and build poor product strategies that never answer core questions. While they may be acting decisively, these leaders aren't aligning with the larger process, or the greater good.

"The people tasked with acting on the leader's vision can get left behind in these types of situations," says Katherine Nester. To her point, the people on the development and design side must connect a leader's big idea to the small steps if they want to create solutions that customers/users need. Unfortunately, any disconnects can prevent a team from putting even the strongest strategic foundation into action.

To align big ideas with actions, your strategic foundation must translate what the big idea means within the systems in which people are working. One way to do so is to apply layers of process with the product vision, to be sure that teams understand how different steps should play out. (Your common language is an example of a shared process.) This helps teams prioritize work, and understand how different steps align. That way, everyone can ladder up their efforts to the bigger vision.

Actions rarely play out mechanically, or flow in a one-after-the-other fashion. What's more, it's easy to get distracted when priorities are unclear. Team members may skip steps if they don't know how different pieces build toward larger objectives. However, if your strategic foundation is aligned, people and teams will understand why certain work is prioritized at different times, and why target tasks and completion dates stack as they do.

Being aligned at the action level is key if you want your project to move forward, while generating buy-in at each phase. Eventually, this may even spur other teams to replicate your process in the future. Here's an example of how a workstream may look, in relation to the action steps you follow:

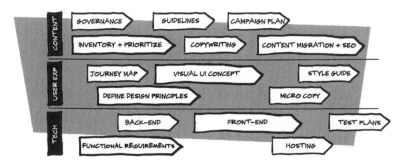

MEASURES: How will your organization measure forward progress? What key performance indicators (KPIs) can you leverage to track, monitor, and assess the effectiveness of overcoming the challenges you have prioritized? Your KPIs might highlight either qualitative or quantitative measures that are pivotal to achieving your intended outcomes, along with the long-term success of the company.

Measuring forward progress and success doesn't always conform to an absolute, as in 'X step will create Y result.' For instance, how does your organization measure product value? Is it in terms of a digital product dashboard and metrics? Is this the only way? Some organizations measure value exclusively by ROI. Others look for a 'wow' factor in the market, improved customer satisfaction scores, or how well a product aligns with value drivers. How does an organization input such metrics? And, what measures truly show that an organization is working toward intended outcomes?

Perhaps the most important question to ask yourself is whether or not you are focused exclusively on lagging indicators—metrics that indicate what has already happened? More often than not, lagging indicators make for poor metrics when it comes to measuring product performance. They tend to fall beyond the scope of what the product can control. Lagging indicators say things like, 'Y occurred, which means X must have happened.' They look backwards, not forward.

Leading indicators, on the other hand, serve as predictive measures, and point the way toward the first step that triggers the next thing you want. For example, 'If X-many users engage with the product at this level, Y will occur.' Leading indicators point the way toward KPIs that product teams can control, in order to create accountability, drive progress, and build alignment. For instance, they may help uncover ways in which teams can change focus, or examine key jobs or tasks that the product or solution must fulfill in order to achieve desired outcomes. Using leading indicators as key measures, teams can see where they're creating real value, and adjust their actions in real time.

"In the Nextdoor platform, we know of three drivers that affect the way our users find value in us," says Tatyana Mamut. In Part Two, Mamut shared her thoughts about why so many digital product transformations fail. Here, she offers insight into knowing which metrics to focus on, and why.

"People who use the Nextdoor platform want to stay informed, make meaningful community connections, and get involved locally," she says. "We absolutely must feed these values into how we measure success." To do so, Mamut and her team look at net promoter scores (NPS). These measure customer experience, and can serve to predict business growth—a key leading indicator. For Mamut, NPS also helps point the way beyond user engagement. "If we were to measure engagement metrics alone, they would look very good for short-term financials," she says. "However, if they're not balanced with what our audience actually values, we run the risk of ignoring potentially bad news for the longer term."

Mamut's point is that, by focusing only on engagement metrics as a core measurement, it could cause the organization to make shortsighted decisions—something she calls the 'potato chip trajectory' of product strategy. "Imagine you're running a potato chip company, and all you do is A/B testing," she says. "You put more salt on the potato chips, people eat more. You put more sugar on potato chips, and people eat more. Then, you put more fat in the chips, and people eat even more. So, you keep doing this, all the while beta testing to see what gets people to eat more chips. At the end of the day, your product is piled with stuff. When people eat it, they wind up spitting it out."

Mamut sees a correlation between the potato chip trajectory, and what's happening in a number of social media platforms right now. "Many are following a similar method," she says. "They are simply heaping features on top of features. As platforms become more feature-heavy, they actually stop serving the user."

Community vitality is another leading metric that Mamut and her team care about. To unpack this data, they look for areas where more members are using the Nextdoor platform, and where Nextdoor's presence contributes to conversations, and the success of local businesses.

"We want to know if communities are becoming more vital, or if they are healthier than others," she says. "We have gathered some wonderful data that shows this is indeed the case. Police sheriffs around the country who have seen crime rates drop, for example, point to the fact that people are using Nextdoor."

Placing a greater emphasis on leading indicators, and including these types of measurements in your thinking, does not happen by accident. It starts with leaders being open to shifting their thinking, and looking for ways to build and maintain alignment within their strategic foundation. They must own the inputs that drive key metrics—not just the output metrics of money and usage—and focus on the value of their products or services. They must also be willing to ask questions such as the following:

- How do we build up the capabilities and competence of our customers/users?
- How do we create something that increases the value exchange with users?

Once again, we return to the product vision. A leader must carry the vision's continuity across every aspect of the strategic foundation. This involves keeping people focused on the right steps, and making sure they don't lose themselves in the smaller details without seeing how everything aligns. It also involves making sure teams believe in the way they measure success.

"They have to feel a sense of ownership regarding the metrics," Mamut says. One way she accomplishes this is by putting her teams in charge of creating the dashboard that measures the metrics they use. "This process sets the stage for ownership," she adds. "I create the framework, and they dive in to build out the details."

When leaders and teams focus on the job to be done, they can pinpoint critical moments in a user's experience. Teams can then use this to establish baseline metrics, experiment with new ideas, test and validate assumption, and refine solutions to create a better result.

In the end, the way you measure success is a highly subjective endeavor. A statement related to your measures may read like this:

> We will rely on **a number of indicators in order to measure success,** and to plan for future updates and iterations. These include the percentage of customers that sign up for three-year agreements, percentage that renew at or prior to their midterm notices, and the percentage that purchase add-on services.

STRATEGIC FOUNDATION ACROSS THE PRODUCT DEVELOPMENT LIFE CYCLE

The process of shifting from developing a strategy, to identifying opportunities, and finally executing effectively across the product development life cycle is not easy. It requires alignment, excellent communication, the right skills, and a culture that willingly embraces change. To get there, you have to deploy capabilities, processes, tools, and resources at the right time.

As a leader, you take on many considerations across the product development life cycle—and they go well beyond deciding what methodology your teams should follow. With a solid foundation in place, it won't matter if your teams follow waterfall, agile, or a hybrid style—they'll be following a path toward success.

Your strategic foundation will enable you and them to do the right things in the right way. And, as teams identify opportunities related to the challenges you've prioritized, your strategic foundation will help you access critical information that validates your work and your timing. Your foundation will also help you:

- Identify employees and/or outside partners who can help create, iterate, and support your product.
- Define a clear picture of roles and responsibilities early in the process.
- Identify and document requirements, and address issues related to business, design, and technical considerations.

As you explore opportunities, you can map out and leverage interdependencies that exist among people, workgroups, audiences, processes, systems, and operational capabilities. Such interdependencies can help bring your product to market in a more successful way. You can lean on them in order to:

- Define and develop stronger and more accurate business cases.

- Communicate the potential investment ahead.
- Explore solutions based on experimentation and validation, rather than assumptions.
- Bring complexities to the forefront, and get a head start on managing them.
- Mitigate risk across every stage of investment.

The product development life cycle focuses on continued discovery, ideation, planning, validation, development, and re-evaluation of a product—from the earliest concept, all the way until the product sunsets.

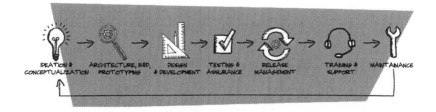

Your strategic foundation allows you to shift into the product development life cycle, while aligning and empowering teams to identify opportunities (i.e. solutions) that:

- Enable the company mission and vision for the future.
- Address challenges in desirable, feasible, viable ways.
- Move you closer to your near-term outcomes and long-term goals.
- Produce continuous iterations and improvements on intended outcomes.
- Clearly define how you will measure forward progress.

Remember, the type of strategy we've discussed throughout this book is episodic. As you revisit it, you can incorporate new insights in real time. This is essential if you want to build and maintain alignment. When you willingly revisit your strategy, you make it easier for product teams to examine their roles and responsibilities at different stages, build clarity, focus their actions, and evaluate the viability of their efforts. This process helps them manage expectations, and track investment plans for each stage. This is a departure from outdated scenarios, where product teams rigidly follow an idea, and rarely have access to a clear or accurate picture that illustrates *how* and *why* their efforts matter.

Whether your organization possesses a risk-taker mentality, or is risk-averse, you will find this approach to be liberating. You can step away from the type of dogmatic thinking or constraints that slow progress, impact quality, and impede smart investing. Even as you focus on outcomes, you'll stay flexible to the reality of different situations. Internally, this approach will help you improve communication between product teams and leadership by using language and processes that build bridges, and align big ideas with small steps.

In any product development life cycle, it's essential to return to your strategic foundation to determine what might be missing. For instance, if you uncover weak or poor product design and/or service delivery, you can take this as evidence of any (or all) of the following:

- You're misaligned at one of the four main levels of alignment (Individual, Team, Organizational, or Market).
- Your current planning is ineffective, or incomplete.
- You lack the internal capacity and knowledge you need to get to the next step.

- Somewhere in your organization, expertise, roles, and responsibilities are not in sync.
- Knowledge is being siloed somewhere.
- Missing disciplines need to come into critical focus.
- Your team is disengaged.

This is not an exhaustive list, but just a few of the issues that may be lurking below the surface of your strategic foundation. Reviewing your initiative throughout the product development life cycle can help you identify and solve these and other challenges. You can also track challenges back to issues with your definition of the current, future, or ideal state. Some potential challenges may be related to the following:

- You lack stakeholder buy-in or involvement.
- There's no clear organization-wide direction and strategy.
- There's a flaw in the customer journey you cannot identify.
- You need resources, or data from user participation.
- You're unclear on user benefits you're trying to create.
- You have not mapped out the technical ecosystem to the fullest extent.
- You don't completely understand, or can't communicate the real business outcomes.
- You haven't identified the right way to measure progress.

Applying a review at different times in the product development life cycle can also help you align your teams, clarify your focus, and ensure that your product is on the right path. Inevitably, you may need to change your course. Keeping this in mind helps you stay open to adaptation—a cornerstone of successful teams and organizations.

Maybe your review uncovers a lack of sufficient or insightful documentation. This is fairly common. Correcting it can be key if you want to expand the breadth of knowledge and understanding across teams. However, ignoring it can lead to silos, where only a small group of people understand key steps. This can lead to poor information architecture, or a lackluster user interface that either doesn't align with the brand, or is missing essential content.

If you follow the strategic foundation process, and discover a few months later that you've been wrong about an essential understanding, it's not a waste of time or resources if you need to go back to the beginning. Doing so might actually save you time, resources, and capital in the end. You're not adding risk when you return to the start—you're actually de-risking your business by aligning essential methodologies of leadership, product management, design thinking, and software development. In short, you're calibrating toward high performance.

How does high performance show up in a product team from the very start? And, how can leaders tap into team alignment through every phase of product innovation and delivery? Part Five will address these questions, with an eye toward aligning teams to win.

PART FIVE
ALIGNING TEAMS TO WIN

Building high-performance product teams

Collaborate vs. coordinate

- A foundation for accountability
- Collective competence
- Collective focus
- Informing feedback via your common language

Decision making and servant leadership

Prioritizing strategy, opportunities, and execution

- Being flexible and adaptable
- Product team functional chart
- Answering how, why, and why now
- Product flows + outcomes
- Product flows cross-functional dependencies
- Measuring product performance

Owning your product

- The case for knowledge management

PART FIVE
Aligning Teams to Win

"It takes a certain kind of person to make connections in actionable ways. They are few and far between. How can we normalize this type of thinking within an organization that wants to create digital products and services? It's an interesting question, because pushing toward a boundary where you're constantly challenged is an uphill battle."

– Christie McAllister, experience research manager, digital platform experience, Autodesk

With many high-performing product teams, the differences that people possess actually help drive the group forward in positive ways. When teams are aligned with a strategic foundation, they are prepared to achieve and maintain high performance as they navigate the product development life cycle, regardless of whether or not they are friends, or even see eye to eye.

BUILDING HIGH-PERFORMANCE PRODUCT TEAMS

Let's return to the strategic foundation, which starts with the first iteration of your product, and ideally will support each product initiative far into the future. In no uncertain terms, your strategic foundation keeps everyone on track. This is especially key when team members rotate in and out.

In this way, having a strong strategic foundation works like a blueprint for team success. It's a guide that helps high performance product teams embrace change, and find ways to improve. Once your strategic foundation is set, members of product teams are ready to:

- Discover approaches that will improve the customer experience across different stages of the user's journey.
- Look for ways to provide more personalization, and deepen the customer relationship.
- Consider improvements that will increase engagement with prospective clients.
- Think of new ways to educate customers, and differentiate from competitors.
- Establish self-service models that will reduce pressure on internal resources, and empower new and existing customers/users.
- Address challenges by enabling workflows across your organization.
- Speed up your time to market, and enhance your product's ability to scale sustainably.

In most high-performing teams, members share a growth mindset, which is essential if you want to capitalize on new opportunities. In her book, *Mindset: The New Psychology of Success*, Carol Dweck discusses the difference between growth and fixed mindsets.[21] Based on Dweck's work, when team members share a growth mindset, they:

- Embrace challenges, and see opportunities among cycles of learning.
- Willingly push their capabilities to new levels.
- Understand that achieving results is part of a continuous process.

In addition, high-performing teams work together as they define the current state, move toward the future state, and arrive at desired outcomes. In so doing, they:

- Listen actively and collectively. In a high-performance product team, people don't talk *at* each other, but *with* one another. There is no *my way or the highway* attitude. Instead, the environment encourages and demonstrates active listening, where everyone is heard.
- Possess empathy, which helps build trust. For high-performance product teams, all opinions matter. Through empathy and trust, all experiences provide insights that move things forward.
- Put energy into achieving focus and clarity. We've talked about clarity since the start of the book. For most high-performance product teams, clarity and focus help people cut through the noise, confront assumptions, challenge perceptions, build momentum, and validate next steps.
- Rely on constructive optimism, which aligns with the strategic framework. I discussed the critical line between optimism and expectations in Part Three. *Constructive optimism* is grounded in expectations. It helps teams push fears or resistance aside, and focus on measurable outcomes.
- Are flexible and adaptable when things change. In many ways, flexibility is the result of the first four attributes in

this list. Any environment that values active listening, embodies empathy, cares about clarity, and puts constructive optimism to use will be flexible by nature. Flexibility is also something that teams foster on their own when they confront challenges, pursue opportunities, push beyond their limits, and work together to manage change.

COLLABORATION VS. COORDINATION

"No matter how brilliant your mind or strategy, if you're playing a solo game, you'll always lose out to a team."

– Reid Hoffman, co-founder of LinkedIn

There is something to be said about the powerful dynamic that forms when groups of people work in close proximity. However, this isn't always the case, especially in an age when more and more people are working remotely, empowered by digital connections.

No matter how or where people work—whether they are down the hall, or across the globe—collaboration is not a guarantee. In fact, many organizations get stuck in a cycle of constant *coordination*, and never achieve a collaborative, high-performing environment. When this happens, the door stays open for challenges, such as:

- Working on different schedules, or having drastically different interpretations of expectations and timelines.

- Being reluctant to claim ownership of the work to be done, and waiting for someone to spoon feed the next steps.

- Lacking clarity, having difficulty tracking progress, and losing sight of who's responsible at different times.

- Hoarding information, especially if there's a lack of trust.

Trust is a huge issue, and if teams are going to move beyond coordination, and enter into a collaborative experience, it is a must. In fact, trust is the very foundation of collaboration, and the key to creating an environment where accountability thrives. To paraphrase Steven M.R. Covey, you cannot collaborate with people you don't trust.[22] Without trust, coordination is as good as things will get.

There are many aspects of trust out there. I'd like to focus on the following four, in relation to helping teams shift into high performance:

- A foundation for accountability
- Collective competence
- Collective focus
- Informing feedback via your common language

A FOUNDATION FOR ACCOUNTABILITY

"Open collaboration encourages greater accountability, which in turn fosters trust."

– Ronald J. Garan Jr., retired NASA astronaut

As I mentioned in Part Two, it's daunting to navigate the sea of unknowns that occur during a digital product transformation. That's especially the case when team members are scattered across multiple worksites. However, when people are aligned through accountability, they can partner in ways that help up-level the entire initiative.

With accountability front and center, people trust that everyone is doing what they say, and teams are empowered to be their best. Even if people don't quite understand how others work, they can trust that everyone is staying accountable to the strategic foundation. This helps teams move forward together.

COLLECTIVE COMPETENCE

"Something you have to figure out is whether or not you have a team that can execute on everything that needs to be done. The ability to execute on critical success factors is a must."

— John Mullins, associate professor of management practice, London Business School

For a high-performing team, the group's collective competence wins the day. This includes everyone involved, across all layers of leadership, partners, and outside support. As people cycle in and out at different times, collective competence is the glue that helps everyone interact, co-create, and solve challenges together.

To take a deeper look at competence and competencies, let's borrow from the classic Four Stages of Learning model, in relation to how four stages of competence create a similar hierarchy:[23]

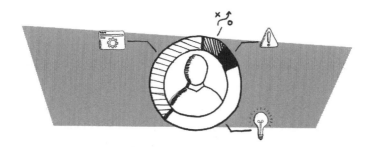

- Unconscious incompetence (having the wrong intuition about something)
- Conscious incompetence (being able to recognize areas where you need to learn and grow)
- Conscious competence (leveling up so as to bring various aspects of expertise together)
- Unconscious competence (an expanded form of competence that experts in given fields tend to possess)

You can view the collective competence of a product team as being the sum of its parts. When teams operate at the level of unconscious competence, they have become masters at their craft.

In a high-performing environment, product teams are empowered to do what they do best. If certain people are less competent than the initiative demands, the group's overall competency will suffer. This can play out at any time in the product development life cycle, and may impact the following:

- Leadership
- Project management
- Research

- Experience design
- Development
- Marketing
- Sales
- Customer service

Unfortunately, leaders rarely have the ability to stack teams with experts who are so unconsciously competent, that they can step back and let things solve themselves. A more realistic path involves focusing on team composition in a way that:

- Creates avenues to learn, share, educate, and coach others up.
- Builds mentorship opportunities within workgroups and teams.
- Pairs juniors with experts on whom they can rely, share ideas, and elevate critical thinking.
- Remains tactical when it comes to making sure people continue to track with the strategic foundation.

Once again, the strategic foundation must be at the center of everything, no matter how competent team members are. When people lose sight of the strategic foundation, entire groups may begin to focus on the wrong things at the wrong times, or isolate into silos.

"In some situations, people start to focus too much on the *what*, and forget about the *why*," says Omri Gazitt. "It's essential for everyone to be able to track back to the bigger *why*, because that's the guiding foundation for everything. Sometimes, you literally have to revisit the *why* again and again."

There are plenty of times when a product initiative takes on a life of its own, or becomes the dominant task for dozens or hundreds of professionals. No matter how many people make up your team, or how you would rate their collective competence, if they lose sight of the *why*, slip into silos, or aren't fully invested in the strategic foundation, then success will be hard to come by.

COLLECTIVE FOCUS

"High-performance teams get together not simply to fulfill a job that someone else has written out for them. They get together to solve problems. Collectively, they understand the problem, and work together to fix it."

— Dan Cable, professor of organizational behavior, London Business School

Right now, teams of people are focused on trying to create and launch the next great disruptive technology. Others are working diligently to help organizations catch up to the last disruption, taking full advantage of modernizing. No matter what shape different outcomes take, high-performance teams share a collective understanding of where they are, and focus together on where they need to be.

Digging out from under the spell of the status quo can be a long slog. Systems can get baked into various organizational processes, and change can be difficult. Plus, many digital product initiatives can seem boring, or at least feel that way at different times. It's especially common when people lose sight of outcomes, or get in a rut where they only care about checking off tasks, forgetting the bigger picture. This is where it's vital to maintain a collective focus.

Regardless of the tasks or details, the results of everyone's work must build toward this focus. Otherwise, the initiative will inevitably slip out of alignment. "It's not so much whether you have a big, mid-sized, or small company," says Omri Gazitt. "What matters is that you form what I'll call a *natural workgroup*. This necessitates that there is more than one person involved. Otherwise, you're just a sole proprietor working in a box. There is a lot of truth to the saying, 'Alone, I go faster, but together, we go further.'"

When people and teams are aligned, collective focus finds its way into the equation again and again. This is very different than trying to force consensus through a pattern of groupthink. Collective focus becomes dialed in as the way that team members and stakeholders approach individual tasks, as if on a circuit that always connects with the larger *why*.

As a career product researcher and lead designer, Deborah Mrazek has been involved in large-scale projects and systems transformations for more than 30 years. One of her first jobs as a human factors engineer involved designing control systems for nuclear power plants. In these environments, the aesthetics were always built with simplicity in mind—the design needed to support speed and functionality in the event of a catastrophe.

"When you're in a control room and something terrible happens, that is the very moment we designed for," Mrazek says. In fact, the guiding design vision for any control room environment is all about rapid response, immediate action, and supporting every aspect of critical decision making. "We were never concerned with aesthetics," Mrazek says. "We wanted functionality and rapid response. That was our collective focus."

No matter what a digital product focuses on, the collective focus must be tied to the strategic foundation. That way, teams and members will align their work with essential outcomes. In Mrazek's control room experience, the collective focus was literally built into the physical space. In some teams, the collective focus will form organically, or build around the way that individuals embrace and embody the strategic foundation.

Still, many teams struggle with building and maintaining a collective focus. This challenge is amplified with long-term initiatives. Luckily, there are ways to proactively facilitate the collective focus of a group. As I've seen in my career, no matter what stage your product initiative is in, a conversation about fears, uncertainties and doubts (FUDs) can be a powerful, transformative way to help product teams remove obstacles and gain (or regain) focus. It can also give people new ways to connect with one another, and inspire proactive thinking and decision making going forward. To lead this type of conversation, consider asking a couple of essential questions to start:

- Can you share your concerns or frustrations about the product?
- What do you think are the biggest challenges or risks?

The answers you hear may surprise you, and can point to a wide spectrum of challenges related to any of the following areas:

- Strategy
- Communication
- Process

- Internal politics
- Technology
- Lack of resources
- Costs and budgeting
- Timing

While these types of conversations can be uncomfortable for some, the end result tends to be cathartic, and ultimately reinvigorating. As teams reconnect, they may even discover entirely new levels of focus.

INFORMING FEEDBACK VIA YOUR COMMON LANGUAGE

"In a project, success or fail, things always go back to whether or not we actively listened at the beginning. Active listening involves taking in different input that customers provide, and combining them with what we know about the marketplace."

– Lindsay Main, head of trade marketing, adidas

The importance of having a common language has come up in nearly every section of this book. It's worth discussing once more, this time within the context of aligning teams to win.

Your common language helps clarify what people hear, and informs how they respond. When you include a consistent feedback loop that aligns with your common language, you keep everyone on the same page. You can think of the feedback you share as a series of micro-adjustments that help people stay focused and on track with one another. In the end, your feedback:

- Becomes shorthand that gives people new ways to connect with one another, and communicate as part of a larger, collaborative unit.

- Increases everyone's competence to the point where you can move more efficiently and effectively as a group.

There are many meanings to feedback—we all provide it, hear it, and discuss it regularly. We offer feedback on projects, share feedback after presentations, and receive it from clients and peers. Teams need to consider feedback across multiple groups and channels at all times. Doing so helps them stay aligned with collective goals.

"Whenever I see organizations miss goals, it's often because they haven't unpacked them collectively," says Omri Gazitt. "Teams are either not aligned with larger, organizational goals, or the lenses through which they interpret goals are too narrow."

Quite often, misalignment in a team's common language is related to feedback—how people share, receive, or interpret it. No matter how misalignment creeps in, if left unchecked, it can fester until it undermines the entire strategic foundation. That's why organizations must focus on their relationship to feedback, in order to ensure that teams and individuals stay on the same page—especially when it comes to tracking goals at critical moments. Aligned feedback will help uncover gaps, and give people new ways to discover whether or not they're on the right page. It could be the missing ingredient that helps to solve issues before they get worse, so teams can engage in deeper learning together.

DECISION MAKING AND SERVANT LEADERSHIP

A team's ability to shift into high performance often starts with leadership. In Part Three, I discussed the importance of servant leadership. It comes up again as we explore what it takes to align teams to win.

"Plenty of leaders still employ a divide-and-conquer approach to management," Omri Gazitt says. Such managers may even encourage team members to silo information, so groups can perfect their part of the widget before it moves down the line. Gazitt follows a different approach in order to foster a high-performance environment. "We distill goals into actionable steps for teams at different times," he says. Doing so helps to anchor teams in the strategic foundation. As they focus on the work at hand, they can pair objectives and goals with other challenges that exist at the heart of a product initiative. This helps team members lean into their collective competence in order to move forward, and align to the *why*. In that way, they gain more ownership over key moments of projects and initiatives.

In the end, this is what leaders want—for others to step up, guide actions, and know when to seek insight and support. This is how new leaders emerge within teams, which up-levels the collective competence of groups, as well as organizations.

The strategic foundation helps to create a system of checks and balances that supports the growth of people and teams. It communicates the following:

- Leaders empower managers to make critical decisions.
- Managers empower their people to do the same.

- Once empowered, team members work with greater clarity and confidence.

This reinforces alignment at the three internal levels we discussed at the start of Part One (Individual, Team, and Organizational), which naturally supports alignment at the external (Market) level. When people are empowered, and play active roles in creating the strategic foundation, delays become less of an issue. Team members know the next steps, especially if they have been working from alignment all along.

In this type of environment, people understand that checks and balances are part of the process, and trust that everyone has set their egos aside for the sake of a successful team venture. At any time, they can check in and ask key questions, such as the following:

- Are we still aligned with our vision?
- Are we on track to solve the problem we've prioritized?
- Is our solution going to deliver the maximum value for customers/users?
- Will it also deliver the outcome we want for our business?
- How well are we measuring progress?

PRIORITIZING PRODUCT STRATEGY, OPPORTUNITIES, AND EXECUTION

Perhaps we've all seen at least one case where a leader or team falls in love with an idea that, in the end, isn't a good fit for the market or the organization. This can be frustrating, to say the least. Did the product simply miss the mark? Was it the wrong audience? Was there a disconnect between how the product was promoted, and what it actually did?

Teresa Torres is a product discovery coach at Product Talk. For her, answers to questions such as these often point back to a leader's ability to listen and disseminate information across teams. "To answer the 'How do we learn from customers?' question, leaders and teams need to define the outcome they want their product or service to drive," she says. "Then, they must work toward driving that outcome."

Torres points out some key insights related to performance. Her process mirrors the one that many successful leaders in digital product transformation follow—she and her teams define the customer and the outcome, then map out the opportunity space.

"High-performance teams identify opportunities that customers care about," she says. "Once they assess opportunities, they look at the impact they will have on their target outcome. A great deal of learning occurs when you're assessing and prioritizing different opportunities this way."

Working from a foundational idea, her teams go deeper into a process of decoding and unpacking different opportunities in order to compare them. "From this solution space, teams start looking at early prototypes, running experiments, and testing assumptions," Torres says. "We delve as deeply as possible."

Applying new levels of scrutiny can be the difference between success and failure. "If something isn't going to work, we learn how to design around a faulty assumption," Torres asserts. "We're not just throwing things at the wall, and wondering what will stick. We're actually finding the path toward a solution that aligns with outcomes, research, and the needs of users."

Working in the solution space should not be confused with trying to upsell, or falling down the *bigger-is-better* rabbit hole. In fact, plenty of times, the opposite is true—you find yourself working toward something sleek, streamlined, flexible, and more cost-effective than what people first wanted. To arrive at solutions that serve customers/users better, you can start by asking some key questions up front, such as the following:

- What is the most appropriate way to solve the problem?
- What is the true impact and opportunity in front of us?
- If we follow X, how much value will we gain from the outcome? How will this change if we follow Y?
- What risks will we encounter if user adoption lags, if resources are capped, or if we run out of time?
- Have we identified the line between *necessary* and *overkill*?

BEING FLEXIBLE AND ADAPTABLE

In a digital product transformation, high-performance teams will be responsive, flexible, and multi-faceted—making it easier for new workgroups and members to flow in and out across the product development life cycle. At key times, people will be steeped in any number of focuses, including:

- Research
- Design
- Content
- Development
- Support
- Security
- Marketing
- Sales

As scope and demands shift, team members will continue to rotate. Specialists will apply new layers of expertise that may enhance the user experience, or increase security. As things change, maintaining your collective focus is vital.

In theory, balancing goals, expectations, priorities, and communication can be easier for smaller organizations or teams than for larger ones. Just consider the communication dynamic we looked at in Part Two (concerning organizational complexity and scale). The fewer people or teams involved, the easier it is to collaborate—or at least coordinate.

Where does this leave product initiatives that spread across large organizations, or pull in dozens of external resources? Again, the more people, the more difficult it is to stay aligned. Therefore, when working with larger groups, identifying responsibilities of every team member becomes paramount. As you scope out the team process, you will want to focus on the following:

- Who is responsible for attending to specific user or customer needs?
- What does the handoff process look like?
- How does workflow align with key aspects of the customer/user journey?
- Are teams aligned and synced up to the point where they can work together with minimal management?
- If not, what steps must you take to create alignment, and a foundation for collaboration and accountability?

When you align strategy, and identify opportunities and execution with proper planning, you are prepared to determine roles, and pinpoint responsibilities. Often, leaders assume that managers and teams already understand this information. As I've discovered, this is where a great deal of confusion remains. Is everyone on the team aligned? Do they possess a shared understanding of purpose, outcomes, and awareness of how the team will measure performance? Does someone have more than one function? Are your expected results and outcomes realistic? Do transparency and clarity exist across the team?

One way to avoid confusion is to stay out of the trap of letting titles determine roles and responsibilities. Instead, follow this practical exercise in order to build alignment, and address issues related to *how*, *why*, and *why now*:

- List each function that makes up the product team.
- Name the person accountable for each function across the product team.
- List any KPIs for this function that you'll use to measure the outcome.
- Write down the appropriate results/outcomes for each function.

The Product Team Functionality chart that follows is a practical tool to help you build teams, and focus on key responsibilities:

PRODUCT TEAM FUNCTIONAL CHART

FUNCTION	PERSON	KPI	OUTCOME
Product Ownership	Stacy	Diagnosed and validated challenge	Clearly defined and aligned product strategy
Product Management	Francis	Defined required team structure	Aligning insights, capabilities and resources to identify and deliver the best solution
Research			
User Experience Architecture			
User Interface Design			
Content			
Solution Architecture			
Development			
Quality Assurance			
Privacy and Security			
Compliance			
Sales			
Marketing			
Customer Support			
Operations			

When completed, this accountability tool helps you assess where you have people and performance gaps, and identify opportunities from across the product team. It makes it easier to spot empty functions that you still need to fill in order to complete your strategic foundation, and arrive at your intended outcomes. For instance, what people, processes, or systems do you need to achieve the outcomes, and accurately measure performance? Once roles and responsibilities are clearly defined and articulated, you can begin mapping product flows and outcomes.

ANSWERING HOW, WHY, AND WHY NOW

Even with highly talented people, the right tools, and experienced leaders in place, completing a digital product transformation can be a treacherous climb. One reason may have to do with whether or not you've clarified your intent. It doesn't matter if your goal is to improve an existing product, or launch something new that fills a gap in the market. If you lack clarity, it will stymie progress, and negatively impact even high-performance teams.

"Surprisingly, some very seasoned professionals get fixated on an idea, and assume the path is straightforward and risk-free," says Teresa Torres. "It's easy to get caught up in the frenzy that says, 'Let's just start building the thing.' I'm sure there are dozens of people in the world right now who are certain they're sitting on the next great idea."

Entire organizations can fall under this spell. Similar to the 'fail fast/fail often' mantra from Part Two, this mindset often comes across as 'innovate or die.' The trouble, however, is that when you follow the drive to innovate without alignment, you are signing yourself up for failure.

"Organizations and leaders will try to oversimplify," says Torres. "They will latch on to a great idea and decide to charge ahead. Melissa Perri refers to this as *the build trap*.[24] People begin to think, 'Oh, we just need to build something.' So they start. Quite often, they don't know what they don't know."

Believe it or not, a little bit of doubt can be a positive influence in situations like these. Some leaders and team members are naturals when it comes to bringing some doubt into the process. Sprinkled around at the right time, doubt can serve as a reminder that you're overlooking due diligence, skipping tests or experiments, or have forgotten about your customers. However, even when doubt helps to balance things out, overzealous teams and leaders may lack critical methodologies that would help them use doubt for good. They wind up brushing it aside, and charge ahead nonetheless.

"Plenty of teams and leaders don't know how to ask the right questions," Torres says. "Worse yet, they're not aware that they don't know this. They think, 'I just need to talk to customers, and the answers will come.' Then they ask general questions like, 'Would you use this? How much would you pay for it?' To them, it feels like they're doing the right thing, but the data they receive isn't reliable."

The same thing can happen when teams start experimenting toward building out their MVP, something that Maria Giudice mentioned in Part Three.

"A lot of teams over-rely on A/B testing," Torres asserts. "They don't understand statistical significance, or the notion of false positives. They run too many tests, but lack a theory behind them. Again, to them it may feel like they're doing the right thing, or that they are using good discovery methods. However, they're getting garbage in return."

Many of these teams know that they need to invest in a different level of research, but they don't always know how, when, or to what degree they should commit to taking certain steps. "If you're building too much of the wrong idea, or building the wrong way, the best thing to do is to stop," Torres says, which reflects a point I brought up at the end of Part Four. Being willing to pause and assess before going forward can help a team overcome the frenzy of urgency. However, this can be a difficult decision to make in a culture where big energy often pushes people forward.

"In that case," Torres continues, "the second-best thing to do—which I think people are more willing to do—is to instrument your product." Instrumenting a product refers to measuring its performance, and carefully mapping out the next version. "Every time you release something, be deliberate about why you expect it to have this or that impact, and see how well it stacks up."

In this context, instrumentation comes in from the product management side. It refers to measuring and tracking key metrics that can help a product team determine how well a product is doing at certain stages. Has adoption gone up? What about retention? What is the impact of a new feature? This process offers new ways to explore data, and get beyond assumptions. "You become aware of how often the things you build have zero impact, or less impact than you expect," Torres says. While it can be a slow exercise, it may be the key to convincing an organization that you're either still on the right path, or that you need to change direction.

The Product Flows & Outcomes chart below allows you to break down your product into the individual flows needed to acquire, serve, and retain customers/users. This is a great way to help team members hold important discussions, and gain a deeper understanding of the product and the value exchange that needs to take place. Whether they agree or disagree, they can talk through various outcomes as they work to solve problems, and move the product forward.

PRODUCT FLOWS + OUTCOMES

PRODUCT FLOWS	USER OUTCOME	BUSINESS OUTCOME
Introduction	Clear understanding of the product value proposition	Clear understanding of the value exchange
Demo/Trial	Access to the product	Shift MQL to PQL by demonstrating how the product will solve the users problem(s)
Sign Up		
Onboarding		
First Time Use/ Setup		
Paywall		
Product/Service (broken down by each individual task flow or job to be done)		
Task Flow 1:		
Task Flow 2:		
Task Flow 3:		
Account Management		
Self-service Support		
Facilitated Support		

In many cases, there are a few essential flows and outcomes that influence the success of your product, as well as other flows. These primary flows and outcomes provide a systematic approach to clarify the needed areas of focus, and areas that will drive results. Here are a few steps to help you get started:

- List each flow that the product must support across the user journey to acquire, serve, and retain customers/users. It can be helpful to think of flows as single or multi-step tasks, or as 'jobs to be done' in order to enable customers/users. The goal is to shift your thinking away from features, and toward users' needs. How do they support the customer/user experience? How do they inform customer/user behavior?

- List the intended user outcomes for each flow. Starting with a user-centric approach to outcomes helps you maintain focus on what users need. From there, you can align their needs with your own goals for the product. This gives you a powerful baseline to challenge, clarify, and validate assumptions that will drive product success. Are you delivering key outcomes today? What would it take to deliver them? What obstacles are in your way?

- The third column focuses on business outcomes. Identify the outcomes that, when met, will determine product viability. Are user and business outcomes in alignment? If realized, do outcomes help move the user forward? For example, through fulfilling the user outcome, are you able to collect the information necessary for the business to deliver greater value down the line?

Steps such as these allow people to look at and understand the broad scope of the product, and the intended outcomes that will determine success. It helps to correlate the relationship between outcomes and your strategic foundation, illustrating the value exchange that needs to take place to drive your business. Using this type of structure can also help you establish a foundation for mapping cross-functional interdependencies, as well as key metrics.

With individual and team alignment in place, and your product flows and outcomes mapped out, the next step is to map the cross-functional dependencies across the organization. Below, the Product Flow Cross-Functional Dependencies chart is designed to help you do this. In many cases, this can extend to strategic partnerships and external dependencies that influence final delivery. It's important to have clarity on these interdependencies as you identify solutions, and explore requisite tactics for delivery.

PRODUCT FLOW CROSS-FUNCTIONAL DEPENDENCIES

	BUSINESS FUNCTIONS								
PRODUCT FLOWS	Product	PMO	Sales	Marketing	Support	Client Services	Security	Finance	Legal
Introduction	•	•		•					
Demo/Trial	•	•	•	•			•		•
Sign Up	•	•	•	•			•		•
Onboarding	•	•	•			•			
First Time Use/ Setup	•	•			•	•			
Paywall	•	•	•			•	•	•	•
Product/ Service (broken down by each individual task flow or job to be done)									
Task Flow 1:									
Task Flow 2:									
Task Flow 3:									
Account Management									
Self-service Support									
Facilitated Support									

To get started:

- List each function that makes up the organization.
- List each of the flows in your product. In some cases, it can be extremely helpful to group or code flows based on the stage of the customer/user journey in which they fall.
- Determine which functions directly or indirectly influence the successful outcome of the flow. What is the role of each functional group?

One way to address the role of each functional group is to break things down according to an internal responsibility matrix, or a RACI scale. For example:

- **Responsible**: Who is responsible for doing the actual work for the task?
- **Accountable**: Who is held accountable for the success of the flow? Quite often, this is also the decision maker.
- **Consulted**: Who needs to be consulted for details and additional info on requirements? Typically, this is a subject matter expert (or group of experts).
- **Informed**: Who needs to be informed of current progress, and of major updates? Typically, this involves senior leaders.

Keep in mind that the person designated as the 'R' should not also be the 'A' for the same flow, unless they have been empowered as such. It is very rare that the person performing the work (responsible) is also authorized to approve the work, or make decisions (accountable).

These steps are invaluable tools that will help build clarity, promote shared understanding, and align your team's focus. As a social contract between team members and leaders, this information will most likely evolve over time. In the process, it will help you address how well your team is aligned cross-functionally, and how well people and teams collaborate across each function to develop your strategic foundation. Addressing these issues can help you identify the best solution, deliver your product successfully, and determine what scaling looks like.

As I've mentioned a few times throughout the book, aligning strategy with execution becomes more critical as your organization scales. When you're smaller, alignment happens almost organically—a few people in a room mapping out ideas on a white board. As you scale, achieving alignment becomes a much different, and more difficult task. "You discover that the techniques you used when you were smaller—the all-hands meetings, for instance—don't scale so well," says Teresa Torres. That's where writing and vetting your strategy—much like Jim Gochee described in Part Three—is critical. That way, your strategic foundation serves as your central documentation, and explains and answers your core *why* and *what* questions.

"Anything you write, by way of strategy, has to answer essential questions," Torres says. "Otherwise, it's just superficial. If people think your strategy is superficial, how will they know what to do when a decision comes? They'll go right back to wondering what the strategy is, and not knowing why it matters."

It's natural for team leaders to want to keep successful, high-performing teams together—or to embed a bit of stability into large-scale product initiatives. However, the reality of such initiatives often plays out differently. People change jobs. Teams evolve. New partners come in and out. As such, keep the following in mind:

- Becoming an expert in anything—especially to the point of unconscious competence—takes time. As the project scales, and as teams and people flow in and out, don't lose sight of mentoring and learning opportunities.
- Even if you have a strong strategic foundation, it doesn't mean that everyone is aware of it, especially as people come and go. Be certain that new team members and workgroups are up to speed on every facet of your strategic foundation.
- Autonomy will always matter, especially if you want people to feel trusted, and to have trust in those with whom they are partnering. When you ensure that new groups and people are aligned with your strategic foundation, you encourage a two-way dynamic of trust.

Once you have defined clear team accountability, product flows and outcomes, and cross-functional interdependencies, you can move into measuring product performance via KPIs. As actionable metrics, they serve the following functions:

- Enable the organization and business functions to keep the strategy on track.
- Spur proactive management.
- Provide decision makers and product teams with information they need to work toward achieving desired outcomes.

Some common KPIs include:

- Activation rate
- Number of active users
- Customer acquisition cost (CAC)
- Months to recover CAC
- Average revenue per customer
- Customer health (i.e. satisfaction) score
- Customer lifetime value
- Lead-to-customer rate
- Total cost of ownership
- Attrition rate/churn rate

While such metrics are valuable, leading indicators, such as those we discussed in Part Four, are what will help you proactively measure product performance, as well as team performance (in alignment with priorities and actions). When you break down and assign KPIs to product flows, you can examine the behaviors that inform product performance. In turn, high-performing product teams can own and use this information to empower their drive, solve challenges, test new ideas, and adapt the product.

"At Zynga, we began to look at revenue per hour, because that was what mattered," says Chris Cravens. "We had monitoring on our systems, which was excellent for the time, but not nearly developed to what it eventually became. Our initial thought was, 'Okay, what is the priority? Do we focus on database servers running hot, or whether or not we're on our numbers? If the servers are relaxed, but our numbers are bad, that's a problem. Or, do we take the opposite approach?'"

Determining which metrics matter can be challenging, especially if you have not strategized ahead of time how you will use metrics. Eventually, leaders must foster an understanding and approach that puts vital indicators to use—for better or for worse. Using information from the earlier Product Flows + Outcomes exercise, you can overlay these metrics in a tangible way via the Measuring Product Performance chart below:

MEASURING PRODUCT PERFORMANCE

PRODUCT FLOWS	USER BEHAVIOR	KPI BASELINE	KPI TARGET
Introduction	Completion	100 per day	200 per day
Demo/Trial	Form Submission	10 MQLs Per Day	25 MQLs Per Day
Sign Up			
Onboarding			
First Time Use/ Setup			
Paywall			
Product/ Service (broken down by each individual task flow or job to be done)			
Task Flow 1:			
Task Flow 2:			
Task Flow 3:			
Account Management			
Self-service Support			
Facilitated Support			

To begin:

- Start with the essential flows to bring focus on moments that make the most significant impact on the overall customer/user experience and outcomes.
- Determine which customer/user behaviors would be a signal/indicator of the desired outcome.
- This signal will become your leading KPI. Using it, you can establish a baseline for performance, identify areas of opportunity, and set feasible targets for improvement.

Through this process, you can see the correlation between user flows, behaviors, and KPIs. It establishes an internal set of levers you can pull at different times in order to improve performance, outcomes, and the impact of your product.

OWNING YOUR PRODUCT

Today, digital products and services have become a competitive necessity. This fact leaves a number of businesses and organizations facing costly challenges they may not have anticipated. Evaluating product ownership is a crucial component of your ongoing and episodic digital product strategy, execution, and continuous improvement. Do most organizations truly own their products? The answer is no. Before I address this fact, let's consider the legal definition of ownership:

> *The state or fact of exclusive rights and control over property (object, land, real estate, or intellectual property). Ownership involves multiple rights, collectively referred to as title, which may be separated and held by different parties.*[25]

According to this definition, most organizations would be able to say that they do indeed own their digital products or services. However, we have to rethink what ownership means in practice, and within the context of digital products. There is a big difference between the perception and reality of ownership in the digital product space. Ownership is typically seen in terms of control. As an owner, you have control of many things, including:

- The direction of the digital product or service, its features, and its benefits.
- How your product integrates into the business offering.
- Designing a best-in-class user experience.
- The business rules that govern the product.
- How data will flow in and out of the product.
- The source code of the product.
- Third-party systems you will integrate with to enable your product and business.

These examples of control assume that you are working in a best-case scenario. However, this is rarely a true representation of what actually happens within an organization, the product ecosystem, or the market. Therefore, we must recognize the fact that an abundance of factors exist beyond your control. When building a platform-minded digital product, it is imperative to ask yourself:

- What does control look like in a rapidly changing environment?
- How will business be impacted when there's a change?
- What happens when change impacts my team, or key team members?

- Will a third-party provider influence our ability to adapt and/or deliver the product?
- What happens if we need to rapidly scale up?

The answers to each question can create a cascading effect. Consider a situation where customers enroll into monthly subscription services that provide access to a sought-after digital product:

- Enrollment grants subscribers immediate, personalized access.
- As part of this, you may have carefully designed an onboarding process that ensures an optimal experience.
- Your onboarding process will most likely introduce them to your amazing customer care team.

Now, let's expand this scenario:

- As product manager, you are assigned to a new product team.
- Organizational leaders have critical business goals, and depend on your product to achieve key milestones. Therefore, you need to get up to speed right away.
- As you dive in and start to learn everything about the product, you request access to all available documentation.
- You are informed that the team follows an agile approach, and everything has been documented pursuant to their interpretation of best practices inline within the codebase.

Who has control? Does everyone across each function of the business have access to the information that's necessary to achieve leadership's goals? They don't. In fact, this information is locked in a format the development team controls. It's not their fault; it's just the way things function at your organization. In the hopes of finding a workaround:

- You schedule meetings with each person who has been working on the product to learn about their insights.
- You also set up interviews with customers to delve into their needs, and assess alignment between the product's trajectory, and the product team's priorities.

Two things come to light. First, you see that everyone has been working diligently. Secondly, you discover that people have vastly different understandings of goals and priorities. Now your concerns begin to grow. You know that success is rooted in effectively moving forward quickly as a cohesive unit. Unfortunately, critical institutional knowledge is locked away with key people. Meanwhile, previous decisions remain unclear, and must be revisited. To make matters worse, you need to scale the product; however, to do so, you also must increase the size of your team. The question of *who owns what* begins to proliferate. Complexities become more obtuse, while new complications pile up. True, the business may *legally* own exclusive rights to the product, but the implications of losing ownership are escalating.

Ignoring the costs of losing control of your digital product is never an option—especially in today's digital landscape. Industries are shifting rapidly. Business models are more complex than ever. Technology is evolving faster than we can track, and competition is everywhere. Plus, when you add the expectations of customers/users to the mix, it becomes clear that maintaining control is vital if you want to avoid falling off the map.

How do you know when you've lost control of your product? It can take many forms. At first, it may seem like an inconvenience, rather than a death rattle. Maybe your product team is unable to take advantage of a new business opportunity. Oh well, you'll get the next one, right? Wrong. Soon, you start to see that:

- You've incurred unintended design or technical debt.
- Your teams lack a complete picture of what they need in order to do their best.
- Team performance begins to flatline, as people start losing time in meetings.
- Work starts and stops in fits. Everyone is either busy re-validating user and business requirements, or trying to manage additional rework of deliverables.
- You're way over budget on a project that's behind schedule. There's no way you can meet pending deadlines with available resources, or manage expectations.
- Finally, you're confronted with the need to re-platform a key product in order to regain control. Otherwise, you'll never reach the numbers that the business requires to survive.

This scenario is happening right now, in far too many organizations. However, it doesn't have to be the case. One way to regain control—or avoid losing it in the first place—is to shift your thinking, and embrace end-to-end knowledge management.

THE CASE FOR KNOWLEDGE MANAGEMENT

Established in the 1990s, knowledge management is the process of creating, sharing, using, and managing an organization's knowledge in the most effective manner possible. It can empower people and processes, support greater decision-making capabilities, and help you construct a library of resources from which to build and maintain alignment. On high-performing product teams, each discipline must understand its role in ensuring that the knowledge management process happens effectively. Often, deliverables must become integrated parts of an ecosystem that addresses the following:

- The *why*
- Context for the product
- The problem(s) it solves
- The outcome(s) it creates
- Business rules
- User flows
- The technology
- Business interdependencies
- Functional requirements

Ask yourself these questions:

- Can you rebuild your product or service with the information you currently have?
- How much would it cost to do so?
- How long would it take to do it again?

A product-ownership mindset empowers product teams, no matter how widely they sprawl. Such a mindset helps you stay focused on solving problems, facilitates your ability to explore insights, and supports you as you deliver crucial solutions. Organizations that embrace this mindset are flexible in the face of change and possibilities. They move faster, operate at greater scale, and are set to increase their competitive edge.

Do you truly own your product? Answering this question can be an invaluable exercise, and help you look at your product and/or service in new ways. Whether the answer is yes or no isn't the point; simply asking the question can:

- Facilitate changes to business structures and functions.
- Shed light on the importance of empowering people and teams.
- Promote sustainable performance.

As you begin to create alignment from the leadership level down, let this be your first question: *Do we own our product?* It may be your most critical step toward de-risking your business, and accelerating the speed of continuous improvements and enhancements. From there, you can affirm whether or not ownership is indeed attainable—and align your teams so you truly own the product.

AFTERWORD

Alignment is the one thing you'll find at the heart of every successful relationship, team, and organization in the world. When developed and leveraged, alignment can create the foundation for unparalleled success, and unlock incredible advantages. Conversely, the absence of alignment can prevent the best ideas from being realized, erode the strongest teams, cripple the most effective leadership, and ruin even the most successful business.

When I first wrote those words, I had no idea how powerful they were. Today, the concept of alignment is more relevant than I ever could have imagined. Product leaders must navigate an unprecedented landscape, and doing so with alignment has never been more essential.

The world we once knew has transformed dramatically since I started writing *Alignment* in 2018. In the midst of a global pandemic, you can see the impact of misalignment everywhere—in our personal lives, in businesses, in our communities, and around the world.

Typically, in times of distress or upheaval, one thing we can count on is the fact that people and groups will be there to help, whether it's FEMA, the Red Cross, or another organization. Now, we have all seen what happens when everyone is in crisis—and when the rules of the game keep changing.

In this reality, our infrastructure, and our ability to serve humanity, become more essential.

As our lives have been transformed, just think of the ways that digital products and services have helped us maintain connections, and create new possibilities. Where would we be without virtual meeting rooms, video conferencing, and mobile applications that help us to be professionals, teachers, and good neighbors from inside of our homes?

We are indeed living in a changed world—one in which we are called upon to create, build, and launch critical solutions. In fact, this new world has accelerated the demand and need for innovation. In that way, technology can continue to unite us, and help us all find the way forward.

Still, many questions remain. How much innovation must occur for businesses to survive? How will organizations know when they have done enough to survive, especially when things continue to change. What type of foundation must they build in order to not just survive, but to thrive?

If anything, this moment is a reminder of the type of value that digital products and services can bring to the world. Through them we can unleash our imaginations, serve as agents of change, and stand firm as makers who are ready to steer society forward. In this reality, the principles of alignment are imperative as we explore and consider the ethical implications, and the social impacts of the products and services we create. Are we truly doing good for the sake of humanity? Can we be better?

Now is the time to explore the myriad of ways that alignment can help us thrive as leaders. What type of leader will you be? Will you become a student of failure, thereby gaining insight into the challenges ahead? Will you commit to serving and empowering others, in order to unlock their potential and invite their contributions? If you have read this far into *Alignment*, then I believe you have already made those choices. The next step is to put them into practice.

Throughout this book, my goal has been to help you realize the powerful advantage that possessing a holistic view of alignment provides. As you do, you gain a unique understanding of what alignment means for people, organizations, and the products we create. Here are a few parting reminders I would like to share:

- Leading with alignment is not any easy endeavor. You will make mistakes. That is okay. Starting with the right steps and sage knowledge will help you succeed.
- Great products, services, and experiences start with empathy, which in turn begins when you authentically listen to customers. Get out and talk to them. Step into their shoes. Confront biases. Unearth a deeper understanding of what drives users. Doing so will help you identify new opportunities, and prioritize your efforts. Start small, create experiments, learn quickly—then execute at scale.
- Get every discipline of your team involved at the onset, and as often in the process as possible. Challenge your own assumptions about customers' situations, their needs, and potential substitutions for your product or service.
- Great product strategy is the foundation for empowering people to make better and faster decisions at every level. It promotes clarity and focus, and when you lead with alignment, you unleash the potential of people, processes, and systems.
- Create and revisit your strategic foundation again and again. Fall in love with the problem, not your solution.

Focus on realistic outcomes, and link them to your business goals—not the other way around.

"We humans are tool builders. We can fashion tools that amplify these inherent abilities that we have to spectacular magnitudes. For me, a computer has always been a bicycle of the mind, something that takes us far beyond our inherent abilities. I think we're just at the early stages of this tool—very early stages—and we've come only a very short distance. It's still in its formation, but already we've seen enormous changes. I think that's nothing compared to what's coming in the next hundred years."

— Steve Jobs, industrial designer, media proprietor, co-founder, Apple, Inc.

We find ourselves at the precipice, and many of the changes that Steve Jobs alluded to in 1990 are here. Our job is to connect them, in order to move into this new frontier with confidence and conviction.

For many of us, the impacts of transformation have brought us back to core impulses: do good; help others; create positive change. As we move forward into an era of massive integration and transformation, alignment is the key to answering the most fundamental questions ahead of us: What can we rethink next? What can we imagine?

REFERENCES

1, Page 27
This quote comes from Jim Collins and Jerry I. Porras, the authors of *Built to Last: Successful Habits of Visionary Companies*. The book was first published in 1994 (Harper Business), and draws upon a six-year research project at Stanford University Graduate School of Business.

2, Page 27
The phrase 'fail fast-fail often' found its way into the technology lexicon, and elsewhere, after the publication of the book, *Fail Fast, Fail Often: How Losing Can Help You Win*, by Ryan Babineaux, and John D. Krumboltz. Published by Penguin, 2013.

3, Page 31
The Speed of Trust: The One Thing That Changes Everything, was written by Stephen M.R. Covey, and R. R. Merrill, and published by Simon & Schuster in 2008. Covey builds a powerful argument that states that trust is the single most critical component for any successful leader and organization to possess.

4, Page 33

"An enterprise that is at war with itself will not have the strength or focus to survive and thrive in today's competitive environment." This quote, from John O. Whitney, professor at Columbia Business School, comes from *The Speed of Trust*, pg. 247.

5, Page 35

How Google Works was co-authored by Eric Schmidt, Jonathan Rosenberg, and Alan Eagle, and published by Grand Central Publishing in 2014. It's a thought-provoking read that explores aspects of corporate culture, strategy, innovation, and disruption.

6, Page 36

Any number of estimates out there suggest the rate of failure for digital transformations to be anywhere from 60 – 80%, and perhaps even higher. A recent article from *Forbes* puts the number at 70%: "Companies That Failed at Digital Transformation and What We Can Learn From Them," by Blake Morgan, published online, September 30, 2019.

7, Page 42

Jaak Panksepp coined the phrase 'affective neuroscience,' which became the name for the field that studies the neural mechanisms of emotion. His book, *Affective Neuroscience: The Foundations of Human and Animal Emotions* (1998, Oxford University Press) focuses on brain-operating systems that organize the fundamental emotional tendencies of all mammals.

8, Page 52

International Data Corporation (IDC) estimates that global spending on digital transformation will approach $2 trillion by 2022. More recent estimates suggest the number will be as high as $6.8 trillion in 2023. Both numbers are based on figures from their Worldwide Semiannual Digital Transformation Spending Guide.

9, Page 53

The vast majority of companies—as high as 89%—have either adopted a digital-first business strategy, or plan to do so. This figure comes from the article, "100 Stats on Digital Transformation and Customer Experience," written by Blake Morgan, and published on Forbes.com, December 16, 2019.

10, Page 85

The book, *The Digital Transformation Playbook: Rethink Your Business for the Digital Age*, was written by David Rogers, and published by Columbia Business School Publishing in 2016.

11, Page 89

Roy Charles Amara was an American researcher, scientist, and futurist, and former president of the Institute for the Future. Journalist Matt Ridley explores the concept of Amara's Law in the article, "Don't Write Off the Next Big Thing Too Soon," published online in *The Times* of London, November 6, 2017.

12, Page 89

Steve Case discusses his view of the various stages, or waves, of the internet in the article, "Steve Case: The 'Third Wave' of the Internet Will Transform Our Institutions," written by

Hope Reese, and published online in *Tech Republic*, April 14, 2016.

13, Page 94
OpenView Partners publishes a regular series of articles on the topic of product-led growth on their website, https://openviewpartners.com/blog/category/product-led-growth/.

14, Page 95
Harley Manning, Forrester's VP and Research Director, presents the concise definition of customer experience in the article, "Customer Research Defined," online at https://go.forrester.com/blogs/definition-of-customer-experience/.

15, Page 114
Clayton Christensen discusses his Jobs to be Done theory and framework at length in a number of interviews, including "What Job Would Consumers Want to Hire a Product to Do," *Harvard Business Review*, October 3, 2016, and "Clay Christensen's Milkshake Marketing," *Harvard Business Review*, February 14, 2011. The Jobs to be Done theory has many positive merits when it comes to cracking the code that drives consumer choices. It's not the only lens through which we can view the consumer-to-product relationship, but it is certainly noteworthy.

16, Page 118
Marty Cagan's book, *Inspired: How to Create Tech Products Customers Love*, was published by Wiley in 2008. The quote, "I see the same basic way of working at the vast majority of companies, of every size, in every corner of the globe," comes from his discussion on the root causes of failed product efforts.

17, Page 128

This quote comes from Richard Rumelt's book, *Good Strategy Bad Strategy: The Difference and Why it Matters*, published by Currency in 2011.

18, Page 128

This quote from Rumelt is cited in a number of online articles, including "The Purpose of Good Strategy," written by Dan'l Webster, and published on *Medium*, August 2, 2016. Rumelt himself shares it in an earlier article, "The Perils of Bad Strategy," published online in the *McKinsey Quarterly*, June 11, 2011.

19, Page 129

This anecdote about Bill Campbell appears in *Trillion Dollar Coach: The Leadership Playbook of Silicon Valley's Bill Campbell*, written by Alan Eagle, Eric Schmidt, and Jonathan Rosenberg, published by Harper Business in 2019.

20, Page 144

Fredrick McKinley Jones was inducted into the National Inventors Hall of Fame in 2007. During his lifetime, he patented more than 60 inventions, 40 of which were in refrigeration.

21, Page 168

Carol Dweck's book, *Mindset: The New Psychology of Success*, was published by Ballantine Books in 2007.

22, Page 171

Covey discusses the concept of building trust in great detail throughout his work, including in the article, "How the Best

Leaders Build Trust," published online at https://www.leader-shipnow.com/CoveyOnTrust.html.

23, Page 172
The Four Stages of Learning model can be found in a number of places online, including https://www.kdplatform.com/four-stages-learning/.

24, Page 188
Melissa Perri discusses the build trap in her book, *Escaping the Build Trap: How Effective Product Management Creates Real Value,* published by O'Reilly Media in 2018.

25, Page 199
The legal definition of ownership can be found in a number of online sources, including https://www.britannica.com/topic/ownership.

ACKNOWLEDGEMENTS

Many thanks to the following people who contributed their time, insights, and most importantly their enthusiasm in support of this project. Through conversations and resource sharing, they were instrumental in helping to shape this book.

DAN CABLE
Dan Cable is professor of organizational behavior at London Business School. His research and teaching focus on employee engagement, change, organizational culture, leadership mindset, and the link between brands and employee behaviors. Dan was selected for the 2018 Thinkers50 Radar List, and the Academy of Management has twice honored him with Best Article awards. The Academy of Management Perspectives ranked Dan in the Top 25 Most Influential Management Scholars. His latest book, *Alive at Work*, was published in 2018, through Harvard Business School Press.

CHRIS CRAVENS
Chris Cravens is currently on the board of advisors for industry leading companies like Zoom, Dell Technologies, and others. He was the founding CIO of Uber and Zynga.

OMRI GAZITT

A seasoned software executive, advisor, and investor, Omri Gazitt has nearly 30 years of experience shipping successful products and services for a number of companies. His leadership roles have spanned across engineering, product management, and leading business units. He has focused on building strong teams, crafting the right strategies, and delighting customers with great products. Among his specialties include running an enterprise business, and hiring and leading teams of great people that focus on cloud, PaaS, IaaS, distributed systems, open source, containers, web apps and services, mobile apps, and distributed development.

MARIA GIUDICE

Maria Giudice has pursued a vision of intelligent, elegant, people-centered design throughout her professional life, during which she has been a CEO, founder, design leader, coach, educator, and speaker. She is the co-author and designer of several award-winning books, including *Elements of Web Design*, *Web Design Essentials*, and *Rise of the DEO*. Under her leadership, Hot Studio, the award-winning experience design firm she founded in 1997, grew into a full-service creative agency with an impressive list of Fortune 500 clients. From 2015 to 2017, Maria led a global team of designers as Autodesk's first VP of experience design.

JIM GOCHEE

Jim Gochee is the former chief product officer at New Relic, Inc., where he ran engineering, product management, and design, and helped grow the company from zero to over $500M in revenue. Prior to that, Jim served as lead architect for Introscope at Wily Technology division of CA. He also spent four years at Apple Computer, Inc., and three years at Connectix Corporation. He holds an AB in computer science from Dartmouth College.

VERNE HARNISH

Verne Harnish is a world-leading expert, speaker, author, and entrepreneur in the field of business growth, who has spent more than 30 years educating entrepreneurial teams. As part of his personal mission to support entrepreneurs, he co-founded Growth Institute, a premier online training company that has helped mid-market companies in over 50 countries learn and implement the latest business methodologies. He also founded the world-renowned Entrepreneurs' Organization (EO), and chaired for 15 years EO's premier CEO program, "Birthing of Giants", held at MIT. Verne is also the founder and CEO of Scaling Up, a global executive education and coaching company with over 180 partners on six continents.

LINDSAY MAIN

Lindsay Main has been with adidas International, Inc. for 15 years, most of which have been spent in product creation, in various locations. She is currently the director of product management for adidas Basketball Signature Apparel.

TATYANA MAMUT

Tatyana Mamut is the chief product officer at Nextdoor, a privately held social networking service for neighborhoods. Mamut works to develop the platform that brings neighbors together, creates safety through community, ends social isolation and loneliness, and revitalizes Main Streets around the world. Prior to that, Tatyana was the general manager/director of product management & front-end engineering at Amazon Web Services, and vice president of product experience, IoT cloud at Salesforce.

CHRISTIE MCALLISTER

Christie McAllister is a people-centered experience researcher and strategist. She focuses on delivering actionable insights, analysis, and strategic roadmaps. McAllister is currently at Autodesk, in the role of principal experience design research manager, with the digital platform & experience team. Prior to that, she held key roles with Scansion, Hot Studio, and Frog Design.

DEBORAH MRAZEK

Deborah Mrazek is the founding partner at Curiate. She brings 30 years of experience to her work, 20 of which she has consulted executives and middle managers to help create and drive design strategy. Mrazek focuses on the intersection of customer value, business benefits, and corporate capabilities in order to align strategic intent with business priorities and metrics, define guiding principles that maximize customer and business benefits, and build aligned and enthused stakeholders.

JOHN MULLINS

John Mullins is an associate professor of management practice at London Business School. He is the author of three best-selling books on entrepreneurship: *The New Business Road Test*, *Getting to Plan B* (written with Randy Komisar), and *The Customer-Funded Business: Start, Finance, or Grow Your Company with Your Customers' Cash*.

KATHERINE NESTER

Katherine Nester is the chief product and technology officer at Ruby Receptionists, where she leads teams that provide the technology that powers the company's live receptionist services. Previously, Nester's work supported the search experience and full customer journey at Ancestry.com, as well as AAA of Northern California, Nevada, and Utah.

JARED SPOOL

Jared M. Spool is an American writer, researcher, speaker, educator, and an expert on the subjects of usability, software, design, and research. He is the founding principal of User Interface Engineering (UIE), a research, training, and consulting firm that specializes in website and product usability. With more than four decades in the tech field, Spool has worked with hundreds of organizations, published hundreds of articles and podcasts, and spoken to audiences around the world. He is the co-author of two books, *Web Anatomy: Interaction Design Frameworks that Work*, and *User-Centered Web Site Development: A Human-Computer Interaction Approach.*

TERESA TORRES

As product discovery coach at Product Talk, Teresa Torres helps digital product teams adopt continuous product discovery practices, including a regular cadence of customer interviews, rapid prototyping, and assumption testing. She focuses on critical thinking practices to ensure there exists a strong connection between what the teams are learning in their research activities, and the product decisions they are making.

INDI YOUNG

A founding partner of Adaptive Path, Indi Young is a professional researcher who coaches, writes, and speaks about inclusive software strategy. She brings depth and breadth of knowledge about people's purposes via the painstaking detail of listening sessions and synthesis. Her mental diagrams, opportunity maps, and thinking-style segments help others organize and activate better support for team members and users.

In addition, *Alignment* would not have been possible without the following people, many of whom have informed, inspired, and motivated me throughout my career, and during this project:

David C. Baker
Nishant Bhajaria
Marc Benioff
Jeff Bezos
Brandon Burchard
Marty Cagan
Jim Collins
Stephen M.R. Covey
Ward Cunningham
Blair Ens
Bill Gates
Mark Gramm
Damon Gaumont
Jennifer Gilstrap
Jeff Gothelf
David Greene

Jake Hammer
Ben Horwitz
Gower Indrees
Aubrey Jensen
Max Leekwai
Kent Lewis
Joe Mitchoff
Ryan Morell
Colleen Murphy
Dan Olsen
Julian Pscheid
Django Radonich-Camp
Marc Randolf
Scott Rich
Phil Riley
David Rogers
Jonathan Rosenberg
Giovanni Salimena
Simon Sinek
Jay Shetty
Ann Stowe
Michael Thompson
Gary Vaynerchuk
Robin Way
Tyson Yeck
Randy Young

RESOURCES

For copies of the worksheets listed in Part Five, and for additional resources, please visit www.emergeinterative.com or www.productalignment.com.

Free for download:
- Strategic Foundation Framework
- Product Team Functional Chart Worksheet
- Product Flows and Outcomes Worksheet
- Product Flow Cross-Functional Dependencies Worksheet
- Measuring Product Performance Worksheet

Additional resources include:
- *Alignment* product team discussion guide
- Symptomatic issues and impacts of product team misalignment
- Product team common language starter kit

ABOUT THE AUTHORS

JONATHON HENSLEY

Jonathon Hensley is co-founder and CEO of Emerge, a digital product consulting firm that works with companies to improve operational agility and customer experience. For more than two decades, Hensley has helped startups, Fortune 100 brands, technology leaders, large regional health networks, non-profit organizations and more transform their businesses by turning strategy, user needs, and new technologies into valuable digital products and services. Jonathon writes and speaks about his experiences and insights from his career, and regularly hosts in-depth interviews with business leaders and industry insiders. He lives in the Pacific Northwest with his wife and two boys.

Originally from Silicon Valley, Jonathon got into the digital product space inspired by the incredible people developing new technologies all around him and the possibilities they unlocked. This fueled his curiosity to understand how technology transforms the ways in which people live and work.

Today that curiosity continues to drive him, as he works to help businesses harness technology. His work focuses on alignment, helping leaders define the value they want to create in a succinct and tangible way; where to focus, why, and what it will take to achieve that outcome. His favorite part is going beyond the idea but reimagining how you bring together people, data, and processes so that a client can succeed.

DAVE JARECKI

Since 2000, Dave Jarecki has provided words in support of hundreds of businesses, non-profit organizations, leaders and entrepreneurs across dozens of industries. His work takes many forms, including brand narratives, presentations, personal narratives, articles, copy, film scripts, poetry and songs. As a ghostwriter, developmental editor, and workshop leader, he regularly supports others as they bring their personal insights and narratives to audiences and readers. He earned his BA in English from Penn State University, and MFA in Creative Writing from Portland State University. He resides in Portland, Oregon, with his wife, daughter, and assortment of animals.

Made in the USA
Middletown, DE
01 February 2024

48431258R00130